The fact that American Christianity [...] ed. It is declining because it has been infect [...] materialism, politics, consumerism, apathy, [...] are warring—to name just a few. As Rick Lawrence so eloquently argues, we are losing the "authentic Jesus" and replacing Him with an "edited Jesus"—a Jesus designed to conform to our desires, our culture, our lifestyles, and our political ideologies. And this "edited Jesus" comes with a false gospel that is no longer appealing to our neighbors. This timely, insightful book offers us just the *antibiotic* we need to reverse the infection and restore the church in America—and our own personal faith—to good health. *Editing Jesus* might just be the most important book you read this year.

RICHARD STEARNS, President Emeritus of World Vision US, author of *The Hole in Our Gospel* and *Lead Like It Matters to God*

In *Editing Jesus*, Rick Lawrence masterfully dissects the current challenges and discrepancies within American Christianity, urging a return to the authentic teachings and example of Jesus Christ. It aligns with all the contemporary research showing that genuine, relational engagement is not only the essence of Jesus' ministry but also the pathway forward for revitalizing the church. This is essential reading for anyone concerned with the future of Christian ministry and the restoration of its foundation upon unedited, relational principles. Its call to action is both timely and necessary, offering a blueprint for reconnecting the church with its mission and with the younger generations increasingly alienated by its current iterations.

JOSH PACKARD, author of *Church Refugees* and cofounder of Future of Faith

This is a dangerous book. And it's an important wake-up call. In a time characterized by people with mouths always speaking curses and spouting slogans, Jesus still asks if any have ears to hear. This book won't just make you think; hopefully, it will make you *rethink*. And *that* can make all the difference.

CONRAD GEMPF, lecturer in New Testament at the London School of Theology and author of *Jesus Asked* and *How to Like Paul Again*

While devouring this book I subjected myself to occasional social-media visits, where Jesus is misrepresented in grievous ways. As I read *Editing Jesus* my heart was simultaneously heavied with conviction and enflamed in hope. Lovingly relentless, the Spirit is gently tutoring me to enjoy Jesus, my Lord. Contemplating my journey through the lens of this book deepens what my heart yearns for most.

DAVE RAHN, professor, researcher, author, and former Senior Vice President of Youth For Christ

Rick Lawrence delivers a refreshing antidote to a diluted faith and a dissolving, lukewarm church in his latest book, *Editing Jesus*, offering a potent shot of the real Jesus for those disillusioned by the feeble state of the church. With humor and insight, he invites us to reconnect with the raw, reality-changing essence of Christ. A must-read for seekers of a deeper, more vibrant faith and a Christianity that leaves a lasting mark on the world.

LEONARD SWEET, author of *Jesus Human*, professor, preacher, publisher, and pioneer of theo-semiotics

This book serves as a passionate appeal for Christians to revisit our "first love" with compelling conviction and striking clarity. It resonates as a modern-day "95 Theses" moment, daring readers to reassess our relationship with all of Jesus. Brace yourselves, for just as Jesus did, Rick Lawrence will undoubtedly challenge you. May God wield this book as a catalyst for revival, drawing a whole generation to encounter the unfiltered Christ, unbound by our human constructs and ideologies.

JACOB BLAND, President/CEO, Youth For Christ USA

With *Editing Jesus*, Rick Lawrence shines a surgeon's light on the cancer eating away the heart of American Christianity. Consistent with the style of Jesus, Rick turns over our tables, willing to upend all our secondary allegiances. In an age when it has become commonplace to co-opt the gospel in service of far lesser causes—some causes wildly antithetical to the character, message, and work of Jesus—this is a wake-up call we desperately need.

MARK DEVRIES, author, founder of Ministry Architects, and cofounder of Ministry Incubators and the Center for Youth Ministry Training

Editing Jesus is a call to the faithful to awaken from our disorientation and recognize that American Christianity has gotten woefully off track. Lawrence challenges us to address our hearts' inclination to reframe Jesus through our own political and self-serving lenses. This book is necessarily disruptive, yet offers us a fresh start, drawing us back to the heart of Christ as He is revealed in Scripture. Both pastoral and pragmatic, this is the work we desperately need to help us rediscover the true "unedited" Jesus and to equip us with practical tools to reclaim our role as salt and light for the world.

EBONIE DAVIS, researcher, coauthor of *Disrupting Teens with Joy*, and youth pastor

I have long respected Rick's unwavering focus on Jesus. *Editing Jesus* is a clarion call for pastors, leaders, and followers of Jesus to reexamine who Jesus is and return to the life Jesus calls us to. My prayer is that we listen to Him. If we do, the church—and the world—will be better off!

JEN BRADBURY, author of *The Jesus Gap*, *The Real Jesus*, and *What Do I Believe About What I Believe?*

EDITING JESUS

***

Confronting the Distorted Faith of the American Church

***

RICK LAWRENCE

MOODY PUBLISHERS
CHICAGO

Unless otherwise indicated, all Scripture quotations are taken from the Holy Bible, New
Living Translation, copyright © 1996, 2004, 2015 by Tyndale House Foundation. Used by permission of Tyndale House Publishers, Carol Stream, Illinois 60188. All rights reserved.

Scripture quotations marked NASB are taken from the (NASB®) New American Standard
Bible®, Copyright © 1960, 1971, 1977, 1995, 2020 by The Lockman Foundation. Used by permission. All rights reserved. lockman.org

Scripture quotations marked MSG are taken from The Message, copyright © 1993, 2002,
2018 by Eugene H. Peterson. Used by permission of NavPress. All rights reserved. Represented
by Tyndale House Publishers.

Scripture quotations marked NKJV are taken from the New King James Version®. Copyright © 1982 by Thomas Nelson. Used by permission. All rights reserved.

Scripture quotations marked (NIV) are taken from the Holy Bible, New International
Version®, NIV®. Copyright © 1973, 1978, 1984, 2011 by Biblica, Inc.™ Used by permission of
Zondervan. All rights reserved worldwide. www.zondervan.com The "NIV" and "New International Version" are trademarks registered in the United States Patent and Trademark Office
by Biblica, Inc.™

Scripture quotations marked KJV are taken from the King James Version.

Edited by Connor Sterchi
Interior design: Puckett Smartt
Cover design: Faceout Studio, Amanda Hudson
Cover texture of photocopy copyright ©2023 by Reddavebatcave/Shutterstock (415299610).
All rights reserved.
Cover texture of scratches and dust copyright © 2023 by Atria Borealis/Shutterstock
(2211170639). All rights reserved.
Author photo: Brad Behan

Library of Congress Cataloging-in-Publication Data

Names: Lawrence, Rick, 1961- author.
Title: Editing Jesus : confronting the distorted faith of the American
   church / by Rick Lawrence.
Description: Chicago, IL : Moody Publishers, 2024. | Includes
   bibliographical references. | Summary: "We need Jesus. The whole Jesus.
   Lawrence explores 8 ways the Jesus of the contemporary church has been
   edited to fit the spirit of the age"-- Provided by publisher.
Identifiers: LCCN 2023056824 (print) | LCCN 2023056825 (ebook) | ISBN
   9780802432889 (paperback) | ISBN 9780802471840 (ebook)
Subjects: LCSH: Secularism--United States--Religious aspects--21st century.
   | Postsecularism--United States. | Christianity and politics--United
   States. | Faith--United States. | BISAC: RELIGION / Christian Church /
   General | RELIGION / Christianity / General
Classification: LCC BV600.3 .L397 2024 (print) | LCC BV600.3 (ebook) |
   DDC 262.001/70973--dc23/eng/20240205
LC record available at https://lccn.loc.gov/2023056824
LC ebook record available at https://lccn.loc.gov/2023056825

Originally delivered by fleets of horse-drawn wagons, the affordable paperbacks from D. L.
Moody's publishing house resourced the church and served everyday people. Now, after more
than 125 years of publishing and ministry, Moody Publishers' mission remains the same—
even if our delivery systems have changed a bit. For more information on other books (and
resources) created from a biblical perspective, go to www.moodypublishers.com or write to:

Moody Publishers
820 N. LaSalle Boulevard
Chicago, IL 60610

1 3 5 7 9 10 8 6 4 2

Printed in the United States of America

Contents

***

Introduction

✳ ✳ ✳

For a decade, my wife and I have created and led a Tuesday night gathering for two dozen young adults in our home. The group's renegade motto is "Pursuing the Heart of Jesus, Not His Recipes." It means we are exploring the person of Jesus, and are fairly unconcerned about "life application." Together, through creative experiences, guided conversations in pairs and trios, visual and audio storytelling, and deeper dives into Scripture, we're on a mission to get as close to Jesus as grafted branches are to their life-giving vine. These nights have been transcendent and immersive and transformational—I'm flabbergasted by the deep insights and passionate revelations these young people put on the table.

And, on many nights, their frustrations with the church also bubble to the surface. One night, after our closing experience, I asked them why so many in their generation see the church so negatively. I've condensed their responses here:

> The church doesn't reflect the heart of Jesus—it's rules-based, not relationally based. There's a big disconnect between what the church values

and what Jesus values. For example, the church is known for excluding people, but Jesus always goes after the marginalized. We are a "come to the table" generation, and the church is a "no place at the table" place. We are a generation that prizes authenticity above all, and the church has become a place of performance—intent on putting on a show. The world is watching the church more than the church thinks it is. And it's teaching things that aren't about Jesus; they're more like TED talks. We don't want self-help—we want Jesus . . .

These "complaints" are really prophetic challenges to the "spirit of the age" in a broad swath of the American church. The young people in our group, all from diverse denominational backgrounds, are describing a church that has veered off the "narrow way" (a passion for the person of Jesus) and onto the "broad way that leads to destruction" (camouflaged legalism and self-sourced goodness).[1] Likewise, after a lifetime of serving the church as a pastor, author, and the poet-paraphraser of *The Message*, Eugene Peterson left us his own prophetic gift:

> Every omitted detail of Jesus, so carefully conveyed to us by the Gospel writers, reduces Jesus. We need the whole Jesus. The complete Jesus. Everything he said. Every detail of what he did.[2]

It would be hard to overstate the importance of Peterson's micro-manifesto—it's a kind of antiphon to the passionate longings of young people who are thirsty for Jesus but know the church-well is dry. The American church is in the middle of a two-decade decline, and the angle of the slide is trending vertical as Gen Z moves fully into young adulthood. One-third of Americans are now "religiously unaffiliated," up from just a quarter a decade ago.[3] Fifteen years ago, Christians outnumbered "nones" (not affiliated with a church) by five to one—today the ratio is two to one.[4] By every measure, religious engagement is weakening and a secular/neo-pagan worldview is fast gaining traction in the culture. Ministry leaders and religious observers are worried about where this momentum is taking the church, and wondering what's *really* at the root of this growing threat.

While there are many surface ways to explain the mass exodus from the church, the active toxin is much harder to detect. Look closely and you'll find it lurking in Gen Z's prophetic indictments. The real source of the church's troubling decline is not its divisiveness or scandalous behavior or hypocrisy or competitive weakness with other cultural influences—these are symptoms of a deeper issue. A deeper issue that young people already know how to articulate . . .

The driving force propelling the church into irrelevance is its propensity to edit Jesus.

I mean, we cherry-pick what we like about Him, or what we find useful about Him in our worldview, and then discard the rest. In Peterson's framework, the church is omitting so many details about Jesus that we no longer have a whole Jesus, a complete Jesus, to worship. And a reduced and redacted Jesus does not inspire worship. We won't "lose our life to save our life" for a "Divine Butler" or "Cosmic Therapist,"[5] the descriptions researchers give for the edited version of Jesus prevalent in Western culture. Translated, we expect Jesus to emerge from His "servant quarters" when we need Him, and stay out of sight when we don't. We want Him to fix what's wrong with us and make us feel better during our scheduled appointment, not live in our house.

When we edit Jesus to conform to our TED Talk sensibilities, or our self-centered expectations, we promote and propagate a twisted version of the Christian life. That, in turn, produces the surface threats to the church—the divisiveness, scandals, hypocrisy, and cultural weakness. Dr. Russell Moore, editor of *Christianity Today* and former president of the Southern Baptist Ethics & Religious Liberty Commission, captures the threat well in his mid-pandemic address to the New York Bruderhof Society:

> If people reject the church because they reject Jesus and the gospel, we should be saddened but not surprised. But what happens when people reject the church because they think *we* reject Jesus and the gospel? . . . What if people don't leave the church because they disapprove of Jesus, but because they've read the Bible and have come to the conclusion that the church itself would disapprove of Jesus? That's a crisis.[6]

Moore is not saying that the name of Jesus is never mentioned in the church—he's saying that the real Jesus, the unedited Jesus, is not palatable to the church. He has been replaced with a jury-rigged Jesus who will be subservient to our preconceived priorities. He's been edited to fit our collective comfort level and unexamined moral assumptions. And because of this subtle recasting, the church is experiencing a painful season of pruning—not a "decline," but a cutting away of what is impeding its growth. Declines among the people of God have no foundation in Scripture, but prunings do. When the church tacitly abandons its source of life (the unedited Jesus), the cutting shears come out. Jesus is explicit about this: "[God] cuts off every branch of mine that doesn't produce fruit, and he prunes the branches that do bear fruit so they will produce even more" (John 15:2). From a gardener's perspective, the Western "branch" of the church is producing shriveled versions of "love, joy, peace, patience, kindness, goodness, faithfulness, gentleness, and self-control" (Gal. 5:22–23).

The dulled edges of the "complete" Jesus sabotage our ability to be in an intimate relationship with Him. An edited Jesus is a fabrication—a false idea of something, rather than a transforming presence. And it's not possible to have a real relationship with an unreal person. We can identify with a character in a film, for example, but we can't *commune* with that character. And outside of intimate relationship, our commitment to Jesus (and to His church) devolves into a "preference mentality," not a driving passion. A preference mentality about our Christian commitments exposes a camouflaged fragility in our relationship with God. And it doesn't take much—a worldwide pandemic, for example—to expose that fragility.

"The pandemic didn't break anything," says Scot McKnight, "but it showed us where things were broken. The health care system was broken before COVID-19. Social support systems were broken before the pandemic. Their weaknesses were only revealed by COVID-19, not caused by it. Church is the same way. People were losing interest long before the pandemic. When the quarantine gave them a reason to stay home, they found out they weren't missing that much."[7]

When we reduce the Christian life from a love affair with the Source of all beauty to a weighted system of life hacks, principles, and values, it naturally produces a weak-kneed faith. Robust moral frameworks, driven by clearly defined principles, can be found in many church alternatives—CrossFit, Comic-Con, political activism, and on and on. "[Religion] is a bundle: a theory of the world, a community, a social identity, a means of finding peace and purpose, and a weekly routine," says *The Atlantic's* Derek Thompson. "Those, like me, who have largely rejected this package deal, often find themselves shopping à la carte for meaning, community, and routine to fill a faith-shaped void. Their *politics is a religion.* Their *work is a religion.* Their *spin class is a church.* And not looking at their phone for several consecutive hours is a *Sabbath.*"[8]

Twice a week, I go to a fitness class at a health club. The club recently added a Sunday slot for this class at 10:15, right in the middle of the "churching hour." And now it's over capacity. People who, twenty years ago, would've been in church on a Sunday morning are now regular attenders at the Church of Bodystep, where they can experience a sense of belonging in a value-driven, principled community of like-minded "believers."

Why make an exclusive commitment to the church's version of systemic morality when there are other (less demanding and judgmental and boring) competing versions? Why add a relationship with God into the mix when we can get "the good life" without all that religious baggage? The warning signs for our present reality were already emerging two decades ago when the newly installed Pope Benedict XVI told more than a million young people gathered for World Youth Day in Germany: "In vast areas of the world today, there is a strange forgetfulness of God. It seems as if everything would be just the same even without him."[9]

Jesus uses metaphors to describe how He sees us—"ex-slaves" and "the bride" and "branches in the vine," for example. But His favorite metaphor for us is "sheep." When Jesus chooses a metaphor, it's a perfect metaphor, because He is perfect. Sheep are timid, easily frightened, and incapable of fighting off any predator. And, relative to our penchant for editing Him, sheep are notoriously *self-centered.* They value their own comfort above all else. For example, when threatened, sheep bully others to the fringes so they can be at the center of the herd, "reducing the chances of their being on the edge and being picked off by a predator."[10] And this, according to Jesus, is exactly what we are like.

We sheepy people see Jesus through the tinted lens of our therapeutic priorities—tacitly demanding that He mold Himself to our expectations, neediness, and existing belief systems. Poet and author Christian Wiman writes:

> One truth, then, is that Christ is always being remade in the image of man, which means that his reality is always being deformed to fit human needs, or what humans perceive to be their needs. . . . Our minds are constantly trying to bring God down to our level rather than letting him lift us into levels of which we were not previously capable. . . . What might it mean to be drawn into meanings that, in some profound and necessary sense, shatter us?[11]

The unedited Jesus who shatters us is determined to confront our sheepy self-centeredness—He does it by saying disruptive things like this:

> "If any of you wants to be my follower, you must give up your own way, take up your cross, and follow me. If you try to hang on to your life, you will lose it. But if you give up your life for my sake, you will save it." (Matt. 16:24–25)

And this:

> "Not everyone who calls out to me, 'Lord! Lord!' will enter the Kingdom of Heaven. Only those who actually do the will of my Father in heaven will enter. On judgment day many will say to me, 'Lord! Lord! We prophesied in your name and cast out demons in your name and performed many miracles in your name.' But I will reply, 'I never knew you. Get away from me, you who break God's laws.'" (Matt. 7:21–23)

Because we are sheep, we disapprove of a Jesus who intends to remake us, rather than the other way around—it's an intolerable role reversal. We want a Jesus who will conform to our existing success narratives, not a Jesus who fully intends to upend those narratives. And so we attempt to bridge the gap between our self-centered demands and Jesus' clear determination to undermine those demands by editing Him.

We edit Him before He can edit us. We recast His plot twists and sand down His obvious (and offensive) rough spots, making Jesus both safer and duller. A quarter of churchgoing teenagers, for example, say they've "met a lot of people who seem more interesting to [them] than Jesus does."[12] Perhaps this helps explain why Jedi-ism—the fictional "faith" practiced by the good guys in the Star Wars series—grew to the fourth-largest religion in the UK.[13] Luke Skywalker has a lot more sizzle than an edited Jesus.

> **We edit Him before He can edit us. We recast His plot twists and sand down His obvious (and offensive) rough spots, making Jesus both safer and duller.**

That's a gut-punch verdict—confirmed by a growing litany of beliefs held by churchgoing, "committed" Christians that are the organic outcomes of this reductionist momentum in the church, including:

- About half believe that "a person can qualify for Heaven by being or doing good."[14]
- One out of five believe Jesus committed sins while He lived on earth.
- More than half believe that the Holy Spirit, the third person of the Trinity and the Spirit of Jesus, is "a symbol of God's power or presence but is not a living entity."
- Six out of ten believe Satan, the enemy of God and Jesus' tempter in the wilderness, is simply "a symbol of evil."[15]

Again, the cumulative effect of this editing is insidious—the imaginary friend of our childhood may have offered temporal comfort in our loneliness but could not be a real companion. And an imaginary Jesus can be no close companion in the reality of our life. Depth of relationship requires depth of reality. Theologian N. T. Wright says: "The longer you look at Jesus, the more you will want to serve him. That is, of course, if it's the real Jesus you're looking at."[16]

When we edit Jesus, conforming Him into the image of our convenience and stripping Him of His essential reality, we lock ourselves into a childish (not childlike) relationship with Him. This is nothing new—Jesus observed the same dynamic among the ancient Jews: "To what can I compare this generation? It is like children playing a game in the public square. They complain to their friends, 'We played wedding songs, and you didn't dance, so we played funeral songs, and you didn't mourn'" (Matt. 11:16–17). Translation: *Jesus, you're not performing for us the way we want you to. So change . . .*

In the chapters that follow we'll explore eight ways we have reduced the weight of Jesus' true presence. We'll discover the lingering impact in each area, and a clear path back into His rich and real presence. Together, we'll humble ourselves in our self-centered sheepiness, so that we can "taste and see" the goodness of Jesus all over again. And when we do, we will discover the "abundant life" He's intended for us all along, and we will learn to walk in His ways.

The Comingling of Kingdoms

✳ ✳ ✳

"My Kingdom is not an earthly kingdom . . ."
JOHN 18:36

'm at a small gathering of academic and ministry leaders involved in a nationwide research project. Our focus is on the forces working for and against "thriving" churches in the US. "Against" appears to be winning the day.

During a break from the presentations, I join a clump of people debriefing the last session. Someone brings up a common cause for concern— the rapid "decline" of the church, not just in attendance, but in respect and esteem. "I've been wrestling with this," he says. "So how do you think this all got started?" There's a pregnant pause, then an academic dean in the group offers a one-word response: "Constantine." Around that little circle every person is nodding their head. They are tracking the trouble facing the twenty-first-century church back to a fourth-century Roman emperor who's often revered as a saint.

After his conversion to Christ, likely a couple of years into his reign as emperor, Constantine legalized Christian practice and signed a declaration returning church properties to their original owners. It was the first in a series of aggressive reboots in Rome's centuries-old persecution of Christians. Constantine's decisions "completely altered the relationship between the church and the imperial government, thereby beginning a process that eventually made Christianity the official religion of the empire."[1] By starting down this slipperly slope, setting the stage for the comingling of the Christian faith with the political levers of Rome, the converted emperor unwittingly invited a cancer into the church. Secular political power that co-opts the language and missional purpose of the church—or vice versa—is prescriptive. It intends to prescribe-by-decree a faith that is meant to be freely invited and freely chosen. And it inextricably links political power with religious belief and convictions.

Jesus does not coerce—He invites us to "eat and drink" Him (a metaphor for intimacy) in John 6, then respond in the freedom that real love requires: "Anyone who eats my flesh and drinks my blood remains in me, and I in him" (v. 56). I married my wife not because I was coerced into intimacy with her, but because I freely chose to commit to her. But the Constantinian Heresy attempts to systematize our relationship with God, using the levers of political power and government to manufacture an "arranged marriage" characterized by a mandated morality. "Constantinian" simply reflects the comingling of state and church first set in motion during the Constantinian dynasty.[2] And a "heresy" is "any belief or practice that explicitly undermines the gospel."[3]

A mandated faith-life undermines the gospel of Jesus and does not lead to intimate relationship with God—this is the "end game" for Jesus' mission on earth, and what He sacrificed His life to restore. Eugene Peterson, in a fatherly letter to his pastor son, calls out the leverage we use to dictate Christian values: "When the missional 'how' is severed from the worship 'who and what,' the missional life no longer is controlled and shaped by Scripture and the Spirit. And so mission becomes shrill, dependent on constant 'strategies' and promotional schemes. . . . But if we are going to live the

Jesus life, we simply have to do it the Jesus way—he is, after all, the Way as well as the truth and life."[4]

The way of Jesus doesn't preclude working through political conduits to advocate for justice, peace, moral standards, and human rights. But it never attempts to take over the levers of political control to establish by force or decree a Christian culture. It never elevates political power above the power of God.

The Idols of Nation-State Worship

How did Jesus respond to power, and how did He wield power Himself? Broadly, the answer to both questions is: *not the way we do.*

From the fourth century to this moment, God's people have been tantalized by the promise of the Constantinian comingling of religious practice and political power. As a consequence, to use Peterson's language, our missional "how" has been severed from the "who and what" we are worshiping. We are lured by a crafty deceit—that permission to propagate the mission and character priorities of the Christian faith *by any means possible* is consistent with the mission and character practices of Jesus.

Psychologist and clergy-abuse specialist Diane Langberg says: "I think in our country, we as Christians have ceased to think that the most important thing that we do is be like Christ, who serves the least of these. That's not what we've been doing. We've been garnering fame and numbers and money and alignment with secular power that makes us look good. And baptizing the whole darn thing."[5]

To undergird and sanction this church/state marriage, a majority of Christians in the US have believed the nationalist myth that America is a "Christian nation" founded by committed followers of Jesus. Yes, representatives in the Continental Congress opened their first gathering in prayer—but who were those prayers directed to? John Adams opposed the motion to begin in prayer "because we were so divided in religious Sentiments . . . [and we] could not join in the same Act of Worship."[6] Historian David L. Holmes notes that many of the Founding Fathers of the United States were "Unitarians, Deists, and secularists"[7] who were "sympathetic" to Christianity, but not particularly followers of Jesus.

Yes, representatives declared that a "spirit of universal reformation among all ranks and degrees of our citizens" would "make us a holy, that so we may be a happy people."[8] And we point to the early appointment of a Congressional chaplain, and Congress's decision to sponsor publication of a Bible, as religious cornerstones in our foundation.[9] But Thomas Jefferson famously edited away all accounts of the supernatural in his copy of the Gospels and did not believe in the divinity of Jesus.[10] And many Congressional representatives, according to Holmes, often opposed the message of the Bible and, like Jefferson, denied the divinity of Jesus.[11]

The Founding Fathers forged a vision for a nation based on Judeo-Christian ethics, but not on the person of Jesus. The Constitution these American patriots created is a governing marvel, admired by the world. Its genius is balancing freedom with accountability, but it is not sacred Scripture. It was written by people who elevated European philosophers such as John Locke, Jean-Jacques Rousseau, and the Baron de Montesquieu, not by people who elevated the teachings of Jesus above all others.[12] And it is not the foundation stone for a New Jerusalem.

The practice of nation-state worship encourages fealty to false idols, just as the people of God have been tempted to do through history.

We vote for the laws and lawmakers that best represent our values as Christians, but we don't entrust political power as the hope of our salvation or the lever that transforms hearts.

Isaiah prophesies that the Messiah will carry the government "on his shoulders" (Isa. 9:6). The Hebrew word translated "government" means "dominion, power, or sovereignty through legal authority." The Trinity invests the Son with the responsibility for redemptive "governmental" impact into the world—the heavyweight mission to "make all things new." We are dependent on the "government" of Jesus, not human government, to transform the hearts of people, which transforms culture.

When we wrest this mission from Him, shifting the weight of transformation to political control, it's quickly obvious that our shoulders aren't big enough. When political structures and political strategy and political goals drive our faith, the weight of governing collapses our weak shoulders.

It's not whether we vote Republican or Democrat or Independent, it's whether we have an idolatrous relationship with human governmental control. We vote for the laws and lawmakers that best represent our values as Christians, but we don't entrust political power with the hope of our salvation or the lever that transforms hearts. And we don't expect coercive tactics to catalyze moral reconstruction in the hearts of people. After reading several biographical books about Martin Luther King Jr., pastor and author Dr. Timothy Keller was struck by the civil rights leader's refusal to use coercive power in his struggle for justice:

The distinction is really about our posture toward ideology—are we worshiping (and therefore submitting to) the unedited Jesus, or our strongly held political beliefs that *require* us to edit Him?

> [King wrote] you can turn your firehoses on us, you can beat us, and you can take us to jail. And we're not going to spit on you. We're not going to speak to you in disdainful language. We're going to love you, but we're going to disobey your unjust laws until you change them. People more conservative than Martin Luther King Jr. said, "The idea of civil disobedience is terrible," but people who were more liberal than Martin Luther King Jr. said, "This idea of nonviolence is crazy." [But King] was saying, "I want the results of the king without the methods of the king—the methods of coercion and power. . . . Likewise, to be followers of the Servant, we [pursue] the results of the king without the methods of coercion and power."[13]

So we ask ourselves, "Which is sovereign in my life—my political ideals or my submission to the values and priorities of Jesus, already clearly defined in Scripture?" The distinction is really about our posture toward ideology—are we worshiping (and therefore submitting to) the unedited

Jesus, or our strongly held political beliefs that *require* us to edit Him? When the two are in conflict, which one "wins"?

When we refuse the Constantinian approach—a comingling of religious faith and political control—we can honor our political beliefs but trust Jesus to carry the weight of transformation in the world. We humbly subjugate our preferences to the lordship of Jesus, rather than editing Him to fit our preferences. And if we refuse, however subtly, we have (by definition) stopped following Him.

The Church Regnant and the Church Remnant

Speaking through the prophet Isaiah, Yahweh reminds us: "My thoughts are nothing like your thoughts. . . . And my ways are far beyond anything you could imagine. For just as the heavens are higher than the earth, so my ways are higher than your ways and my thoughts higher than your thoughts" (Isa. 55:8–9). Nowhere is this contrast more obvious than in the way so many contemporary Christians think about power and practice it in the real world. We have invested ourselves in political salvation narratives, on both the right and the left, because we believe real power is best expressed through human systems of control, not through the lifestyle of submission, sacrifice, and Spirit-dependence Jesus taught and modeled. For example, most Americans think the founders intended for the US to be a prescribed "Christian nation," and almost half think it *should be*. This belief opens wide the door to the excesses of those who believe in Christian governance, not merely Christian influence.[14]

Just two days before the 2020 US election, in a charged cultural atmosphere frothed by division, *Christianity Today* president Timothy Dalrymple published a widely talked-about opinion piece highlighting the two approaches to power prevalent in the church—the "Church Regnant" and the "Church Remnant." Those who identify with the first camp, says Dalrymple, "place a higher value on the acquisition and use of political power. . . . Winning political power means protecting the Christian way of life and sowing seeds of truth and goodness into culture, and thus bringing God's blessing upon the land. Losing political power means the culture spirals into deepening immorality and untruth, eroding the foundations of society and leading to greater suffering for all." In contrast, for those in the Church Remnant, "the kingdom of God is less about the acquisition of power than the divestment of power, laying down our rights and privileges as Christ did (Philippians 2) in order to serve the powerless. In other words, Christendom is not the kingdom, and representing Christendom is not the same as representing Christ."[15]

Those who push the priorities of the Church Regnant intend to use human systems of control to force an outcome that God seems reluctant to bring about. For example, when Christian morals and ethics are commonly rejected in the culture, those in the Church Regnant believe they can reverse that momentum by mandating Christian goverance. So a change in who governs, and how they govern, is the answer.

We believe real power is best expressed through human systems of control, not through the lifestyle of submission, sacrifice, and Spirit-dependence Jesus taught and modeled.

People who invest in this strategy tacitly fall into the mistake made by Abraham in the Old Testament. Remember, Abraham's defining act of disobedience is his impatience over the promises of God—he's been told he will have a family and land, but late into his life he has neither. So, with his wife Sarai, he decides to circumvent God's delayed provision and exercise human control over the promised outcome, "going into" Sarai's Egyptian maid Hagar to produce the heir God has not delivered (Gen. 16).

Likewise, many in the church today believe it's imperative that we "birth" a Christianized culture using the "Hagar" of political control. For example, those who identify as the most active churchgoers, holding to a "literal" interpretation of the Bible, believe the US government should "advocate Christian values," "fund faith-based organizations," and "allow prayer in schools."[16] Christian cominglers don't want the government to broadly advance religious beliefs and practices through political control unless, of course, those religious beliefs are solely Christian. "Allowing" prayer in school is a misnomer, for example—no one is preventing people from praying in school. But supporters of prayer in school want teachers and administrators to have a green light to lead students in Christian prayer, though the student population is diverse along the religious continuum. In effect, that means a Christian teacher praying a Christian prayer can require all kids to participate (or at least be exposed to) a Christian faith practice. There's just no precedent in Jesus for this kind of mandated participation. The opposite is true—Jesus invites but never forces faith practices. Why? Because followers *choose* to follow. They are not *required* to follow.

Some in the Church Regnant advocate for mandated Christian practices because they are weary of God's slow-moving reclamation project among humankind. If people will not wake up and adopt God's values and priorities, they argue, then we need to force what He seems unwilling to force. This is the subtle shift into the Constantinian Heresy—and it's what makes its contemporary form, the Christian nationalism ideology, also a heresy.

According to a definitive study on the prevalence of this ideology among Americans, about a third of the population are fully or partially supportive of it,[17] and that percentage skyrockets to two-thirds among white evangelical Protestants.[18] It is, simply, a power-grab camouflaged by religious language and symbols—an ideology that assumes its foundation in the person of Jesus, but does not reflect the way of Jesus.

So, to resolve the dissonance between Christian-y tactics and the model of Jesus, the Church Regnant bends the words and ways and symbols of Jesus to support a worldview that *seems* Christian but is actually secular (or humanist) at its core—"the Kingdom of God without the King," as Australian pastor and cultural philosopher Mark Sayers describes it.[19] It's the advancement of an ideal Christian/political culture with an edited, reduced Jesus as its figurehead, but not as its Lord.

Tim Smith, formerly on the pastoral staff of Mars Hill Church in Seattle and eyewitness to the rampant abuse of religious power that led to the church's spectacular implosion, says: "If Jesus came today in America, we would do to Him the same thing that Jewish leaders did back in His day, because we have a counterfeit version of the faith based on other values than what Jesus has. And if Jesus showed up, He wouldn't keep us in power the way we want to be, and we would kill him. . . . The Church of His name has just become so distorted and deceived, and has adopted so many values that are contrary to Him. We need to follow Jesus—[that's] what we need to do."[20]

The Church as a "Political Tool"

In the spring of 2022, Andy Stanley, pastor of arguably the most influential evangelical church in North America (Atlanta's North Point Community Church), grabbed headlines after this incendiary quote from his book *Not in It to Win It* surfaced: "The moment our love for or concern for country takes precedence over our love for people in our country, we are off mission. When saving America diverts energy, focus, and reputation away from saving Americans, we no longer qualify as the ekklesia [church]. We're merely political tools. A manipulated voting demographic. A photo op. . . . We give up the moral and ethical high grounds."[21]

Stanley is merely restating theological orthodoxy ("You shall have no other gods before Me"—Ex. 20:3 NASB), but it's headline material because he's speaking from "the belly of the beast." He's a lightning-rod evangelical leader exposing a twisted departure from the historic values and priorities of his own movement. He is firing a warning flare over the heads of those who have repurposed the way of Jesus into a political power narrative.

Researcher and political scientist Ryan Burge says 40 percent of those who identify as "evangelical" actually attend church once a year or less.[22] If we use churchgoing as a surface marker for commitment, this means "evangelical" has devolved from a statement of belief into a political label, propagating the cancer brought on by the Constantinian Heresy. And that cancer is eating away at the church's mission, passion, and purpose—undermining Jesus' prayer that His body would "be one as we are one" (John 17:22). The apostle Paul knew the church would be vulnerable to this attack, especially if its "immune system" was weakened by religious propaganda and division: "But if you are always biting and devouring one another, watch out! Beware of destroying one another" (Gal. 5:15).

While the source and symptoms of the comingling cancer are overt on the Christian right, the left has its own more subtle and dispersed expression. Serene Jones, president of Union Theological Seminary, says: "Progressive Christians feel very strongly about the central idea of the fundamental equality of human beings, the preciousness of the Earth and economic justice—that we all deserve to be treated equally and to have the conditions for our flourishing as the baseline starting point for our lives together."[23]

These theological pillars have seeped into the Christian left's political positions on abortion, socialism, immigration policy, LGBTQ rights, wealth disparity, and climate change. The rhetoric around these issues, like the rhetoric coming from the evangelical right, promotes only those aspects of Jesus that fit a certain political salvation narrative. Jesus engages people with shocking kindness and inclusion, but He's also brusque to some ("It isn't right to take food from the children and throw it to the dogs"—Mark 7:27) and exclusionary to many ("I will declare to them, 'I never knew you; depart from Me'"—Matthew 7:23 NKJV). (More on the progressive wing of the church and its aversion to the hard edges of Jesus in chapter 2.)

For those who've been swept up into this heresy, salvation is a party platform that uses Jesus as a means to an end. Russell Moore says: "When 'winning' is the primary objective, one can justify any allegiance, immorality, or idolatry as 'necessary' to achieve the goal. Can that sometimes produce political or social 'wins'? Yes—in the same way that an embezzling banker can get rich or an adulterous spouse can have sexual pleasure. But what is at the end of all that? What happens to *you*?"[24] Jesus has told us what will happen when we twist the truth about Him to get what we want: "What do you benefit if you gain the whole world but lose your own soul?" (Mark 8:36).

In decoupling itself from the priorities and practices of Jesus, the Church Regnant has cut itself off from the lifeblood of morality. A branch cut from a tree will still look like a branch, even (temporarily) have the feel of a living thing, but over time, with its source of life gone, it will shrivel into deadness. We don't "win" anything when we use religious language to leverage our political goals and excise the Spirit, value system, and intentions of Jesus from the equation.

When the Barna Group asked a cross-section of Americans if they could think of a *single* positive contribution the Christian church has made to society, one-quarter said they couldn't (even though nearly every outreach to the poor and needy in our society can be traced back to Christian roots).[25] Much of America suspects that our shining "city on a hill" is morally bankrupt—the sobering consequence of a church that has forgotten its mission and ignored Jesus' clear example of political restraint. Abraham's act of disobedience with Hagar leads to enmity, betrayal, war, and division—and we are now experiencing a church whose fixation on secular power has led to enmity, betrayal, war, and division. Those who have woven political power into the threads of the gospel say they are Christians, but they are not following Jesus. Because a passion for Christendom is not the same as a passion for Christ.

David French, the respected conservative political commentator and *New York Times* columnist, says: "To be sure, some of the best people in public life proclaim the name of Christ. But so do some of the worst. While some of the most important fights for justice have been led by Christians . . . some of the most destructive political and cultural forces have been loudly and proudly led by Christians as well."[26]

How Jesus Relates to Political Power

After the feeding of the five thousand on the shore of the Sea of Galilee, the astonished crowd works itself into a political frenzy over Jesus: "Surely this man is the Prophet we've been expecting" (John 7:40). And Jesus, recognizing the political forces building like a tidal wave about to wash over Him, and aware the crowd intends to install him as king by force, "slips away in the hills by himself."

With the prospect of a political/religious comingled movement laid before Him, Jesus *escapes*. Why? Because the kingdom He is inaugurating is focused on influencing the heart, not secular levers of power. He will transform culture by transforming individuals—inviting them into the beauty of His presence, fueling their passion, then scattering them like salt to season the world.

"You are the salt of the earth," Jesus tells the people of God. "But what good is salt if it has lost its flavor?" (Matt. 5:13). Salt is a small thing that alters the experience of a big thing. The followers of Jesus cannot assimilate with the ways of the world without losing their ability to season. Jesus' yeast metaphor works the same way: "The Kingdom of Heaven is like the yeast a woman used in making bread," He says. "Even though she put only a little yeast in three measures of flour, it permeated every part of the dough" (Matt. 13:33).

Those who support and further the goals of God's kingdom comingled with the kingdom of political power—who advocate for a government-mandated adherence to Christian religious expression—are trying to make salt the meal, not the seasoning. They are baking a loaf of bread using yeast as the main ingredient. The church is meant to be a redemptive outpost in the wider culture, never the dominant "ingredient" in that culture. Salt remains small, though its power to season is outsized and profound. That's the point of Jesus' reference. He could have said the church is meant to be the "flour" of every culture—the primary ingredient. But He doesn't. When we try to mandate adherence to the values of "the Kingdom of Heaven," making it the dominant ingredient, it's no longer salt used to season. It's no wonder the wider culture is gagging on what the Christian nationalist ideology is serving up—comingling the kingdom of God with the kingdom of political power is like stuffing its mouth with salt.

On trial before Pilate, hours away from His death on a cross, Jesus says: "My Kingdom is not an earthly kingdom. If it were, my followers would fight to keep me from being handed over to the Jewish leaders. But my Kingdom is not of this world" (John 18:36). The leaders of earthly kingdoms fight for power, consolidate power, and scheme for political survival. Jesus does none of that. In the garden of Gethsemane, Jesus rebukes Peter's panicked attempt to defend Him. Peter swings his sword at the armed mob that comes to arrest Jesus, cutting off the ear of the high priest's slave (John 18:10). If Jesus intends to lead a political insurrection, Peter's bravado will be hailed as the spark that set off a revolution. Instead, at a moment when the need for expected forms of power and control seem obvious, Jesus rejects them. And He restores the harm caused by Peter's attempted rebellion by healing the man's ear.

A kingdom "not of this world" does not use the sword of secular power to defend or advance its mission by force—in his rebuke of Peter, Jesus says: "Put your sword back into its sheath. Shall I not drink from the cup of suffering the Father has given me?" (John 18:11). Jesus is rebuking his friend for trying to leverage human power to further the kingdom of God, rather than accepting the self-sacrificing path of transformation that He is determined to walk.

Before Constantine, the church was mercilessly persecuted and the "cost of discipleship" was real, not rhetorical. The followers of Jesus drank from His same "cup of suffering." And, under this great duress, the gospel of Jesus spread throughout the world, upending every institution from the inside out. John Ortberg writes: "Normally when someone dies, their impact on the world immediately begins to recede. But . . . Jesus' impact was greater a hundred years after his death than during his life; it was greater still after five hundred years; after a thousand years his legacy laid the foundation for much of Europe; after two thousand years He has more followers in more places than ever."[27] All of this happened because the church operated as salt and yeast in the wider culture. But the attempted Christian elevation of secular power over the inside-out transformation of the human heart undermines this salty kingdom-of-God strategy—a defeat masquerading as victory.

In Iran, for so long a notoriously harsh environment for those who publicly follow Jesus, more Persian people have come to faith in the last ten years than in the last ten centuries. For scores of Iranian Christians living under a repressive regime that punished and martyred believers, drinking from the "cup of suffering" wiped away the circumstantial rewards those in the West expect to receive from living the Christian life. What's left is the beauty of Jesus Himself. David Yeghnazar, a leader in the "underground" Iranian church, describes what he saw in the courageous leaders who first risked their lives to share their faith in the face of persecution: "First of all they were deeply in love with Jesus, that was very evident. . . . If you really want to build something, first of all, it starts with loving Jesus. They had an absolute conviction that no matter what the opposition was, no matter what the obstacle was, that He could make a way. . . . That kind of faith that comes out of love, really."[28]

Political power could never leverage the kind of cultural change that has accompanied this improbable Christian renewal—put another way, spiritual revivals are never catalyzed by political control. Instead, in Iran, average people are simply sharing the love they are experiencing with their average friends and neighbors. That's how the church experiences exponential growth—one by one and inside-out is the Jesus way.

And so the way of the unedited Jesus invites us, simply, to sheath our swords and reject political power as a controlling means to the kingdom of God's redemptive ends. The Church Regnant is not just the least-preferred option between two factions of the church; its priorities and methodology are *never* modeled by Jesus.

So, back to the questions that frame the beginning of this chapter: *How does Jesus respond to power, and how does He wield power?* Here's a thumbnail guide, drawn from just three encounters Jesus has with religious and secular power in Matthew 17, John 8, and John 18.

Jesus Engaging Power	Jesus Responding to Power	Jesus Exercising Power
In **John 18:28-40**, soldiers take Jesus to the Roman governor, Pilate, to be "tried" and judged for execution. Pilate asks if He is "king of the Jews," but Jesus turns the tables and asks if this is his own question, or if others have "planted" it. He confirms to Pilate that He is a king, but His kingdom "is not an earthly kingdom." And He testifies to Pilate that He "came into the world to testify to the truth," but Pilate responds, "What is truth?"	• Jesus respects established authorities and power structures but reminds those who entrust themselves to secular power that there is a superseding authority that transcends them all. • Jesus is not impressed with power or leveraged by the threat of power.	• Jesus invites all to participate in His mission, emphasizing that His "currency" is tied to the level of trust we exercise, not the thickness of our power-wallet. • Jesus is secure in His power, and therefore free to expose the insecurities that are the true source of most secular/human expressions of power: "Is this your own question, or did others tell you about me?"

Jesus Engaging Power	Jesus Responding to Power	Jesus Exercising Power
In **John 8:1–11**, a woman is set up by a group of conspiring religious leaders so that she is caught in the act of adultery. They bring her to Jesus to test whether He will give His stamp of approval to her execution, as Jewish law requires. Instead, Jesus subverts their plan with: "Let the one who has never sinned throw the first stone!"	• Jesus discerns between expressions of power that uphold the values of the kingdom of God and those that are corrupt—He embraces the first and calls out the second. • Jesus is an expert at removing the fuel rod from the power-reactors of culture. When secular power is building toward coerced religious goals, He siphons away the energy that is animating those sources of power.	• Jesus reorders the established authority structures by targeting the heart instead, elevating the power of the heart above the power of the fist. • Jesus surfaces and celebrates the intrinsic dignity of all, stripping Himself of the trappings of power to remove any impediments to relationship.
In **Matthew 17:24–27**, the Temple tax collectors show up where Jesus and Peter are staying in Capernaum, asking if they have paid the tax they owe for the Temple's upkeep. Jesus instructs Peter to go to the shore and catch a fish—in the fish's mouth will be a coin that pays what they both owe.	• Jesus upends surface expressions of power, intentionally modeling what's *actually* powerful. • Jesus responds to coercive, denigrating expressions of power in the "opposite spirit" of those He's engaging, undermining the foundations of that power.	• Jesus undermines the exclusivity of privilege, deconstructing hierarchies of power and flattening assumptions about roles and responsibilities. • Jesus does not usurp secular power; He outwits it, redirecting it for His own purposes.

To reiterate, the way of Jesus doesn't preclude working through political conduits to advocate for justice, peace, moral standards, and human rights. But it never attempts to take over the levers of political control to establish by force or decree a Christian culture. It never elevates political power above the power of God. In fact, we have many examples of the Trinity thwarting and intentionally undermining human foundations of strength in those who intend to advance His mission by force.

In the Old Testament story of Gideon (Judg. 7), God taps a most un-likely leader to lead a ragtag, underwhelming army against an alliance of enemies led by the ruthless Midianites. The Israelites manage to gather thirty thousand "warriors," but God pinpoints a problem: "You have too many warriors with you. If I let all of you fight the Midianites, the Israelites will boast to me that they saved themselves by their own strength" (v. 2). So He releases all those who are "timid or afraid," and two-thirds of the army abandons the fight. But ten thousand is still too many, so God reduces the force to a ridiculous three hundred men, who promptly rout and destroy the vast armies camped in the valley below.

In the New Testament we see the same pattern. Three times the apostle Paul begs Jesus to remove a threat to his strength (metaphorically, a "thorn in his side"), and three times Jesus refuses with this terse-but-loving response: "My grace is all you need. My power works best in weakness" (2 Cor. 12:9). In both examples, the Trinity is sending a clear message to those of us who can't resist the temptation to exercise our own strength when God's inside-out strategy for transformation seems weak in comparison: *It's best for everyone to rely on My power, not yours.*

Why is this true? Human beings worship power. When we are enamored of our own strength, we are functionally worshiping ourselves, feeding the fundamental temptation already exposed in the garden: "You will be like God." Adam and Eve are banished from the garden not as punishment, but as rescue. The path they have started down will lead to their destruction. We cannot worship God and also worship ourselves—it's one or the other. And when we choose to worship our own power and agency above God, installing ourselves as gods, we cut ourselves off from our only source of life. Jesus reminds us of the mission behind His counterinsurgency in our lives: "The thief's purpose is to steal and kill and destroy. My purpose is to give them a rich and satisfying life" (John 10:10).

Walking the Way of (the Unedited) Jesus

What will it look like if we walk in the way of the unedited Jesus, refusing to comingle the kingdom of God with the kingdom of secular power? Here are a few possibilities:

1. Emphasize what we're for, and look for ways to plant God's goodness in the world.

Several years ago I was speaking at a conference for denominational ministry leaders—they came from more than twenty countries around the world. I divided the room in half and had ministry leaders on each side find a partner. Then I challenged pairs on one side to list things the church is *against*, and pairs on the other side to list things the church is *for*. After two minutes, I had the pair with the longest list on both sides read them aloud. Then I asked the whole group: "Which list would people who are outside the church be more familiar with?" They had no doubt: "Against!" they screamed. Here's the sad fact: *About the only thing most people know about Christians today is what we're against.* Salt *adds* to the flavor of the meal (or culture); and when it's added in the right amount it brings out the goodness of the food—it doesn't *replace* the food.

Likewise, David French says: "Early church fathers were far, far more concerned with the faith and virtue of the church than the maladies of the Romans. Indeed, we forget a fundamental truth—our own maladies often make us unable to see the world clearly. Or, as Jesus said, 'You hypocrite, first take the plank out of your own eye, and then you will see clearly to remove the speck from your brother's eye.'"[29] Put another way, we pay attention to the salt we're adding to the meal—our "seasoning"—more than we complain about how bad the food is, or how incompetent the "chefs" who made the food are. We pay attention to our own brokenness and pursue healing through our dependent relationship with Jesus. And as we experience healthy growth in ourselves, we offer our salt as seasoning in our culture and context.

Rather than obsessing about fixing our broken world by investing our faith in political power to get things set right, we nurture what we are for—our own "faith and virtue"—rather than what we're against—"the maladies of the Romans [pursuing salvation strategies that depend upon political power]."

Christians have been working to abolish slavery for centuries—an "against" that seems self-evident. At the turn of the nineteenth century, many around the world began to see the economic downside of the slave trade and how it undermined free-market economic ideals and tamped down economic growth in the world. At the same time, Christians and "enlightened" intellectuals began railing against slavery as a moral evil. These forces combined and, eventually, led to a political "win"—laws were passed in Europe and America making the slave trade illegal. But more than two centuries later, we still have more than fifty million people living in slavery[30]—more than at any other time in history. It's evident that political solutions can lead to changes in the law, but they don't necessarily leverage changes in the heart.

Philosopher John Stuart Mill, a member of the British Parliament at the height of its abolitionist momentum, observed that abolition was a result not of "any change in the distribution of material interests," but rather "by the spread of moral convictions." Mill wrote: "It is what men think that determines how they act."[31] What we think, and therefore what we do, is primarily influenced by a change of heart, not political or governmental mandates. This is why Jesus focuses on heart-change, leading to a change in the way we think, rather than focusing on political solutions to the world's ills.

In Matthew 13, He tells the parable of the wheat and the weeds—the meaning, He explains to His disciples, is multilayered. The "good seeds" He's planted in the world represent the values and priorities and culture of His kingdom—the "people of the Kingdom." The "bad seeds" planted among the wheat represent the values and priorities and culture of the "evil one"—the forming influence of the world's denigrating lies. Jesus warns against the "farmer's workers" [His followers] pulling the weeds when they see them. Instead, He says, let the weeds grow for now, because He will take care of them later. Meanwhile, focus on growing and nurturing the good stuff—what we're "for" in people and culture (the wheat). Gardeners know, by the way, that fertilizing and nurturing healthy plants is a "natural weed management"—thriving plants choke out the sources of life weeds depend upon.

So, to guide our everyday interactions and missional intentions in the culture, we consider WWJF—"What Was Jesus For"? Of course, every "for" has a corresponding "against," but we have way overinvested in our againsts and way underinvested in our fors. Jesus wants us to be wheat farmers by trade, not weed pullers. His Sermon on the Mount in Matthew 5, 6, and 7 is a "shock and awe" unveiling of what people who live out the values of the kingdom of God promote and practice: love your enemies, treat others with dignity, live out your relationship with God with humility and integrity, forgive others while recognizing your own brokenness, work for justice, give the good things you have to give, invest in others' well-being more than you invest in your own wealth, and walk the narrow road in life that honors the kingdom above all else.

To follow Jesus means we abide in His presence so regularly, so deeply, that His values infect and overtake our values—we naturally nurture the wheat in ourselves, in our communities, and in our world. The values Jesus spotlighted in His Sermon on the Mount are the fruit of our abiding dependence on Him. We cannot "work up" this kind of transformational goodness—we can only attach ourselves to its source and make ourselves a conduit for it to flow into the world.

---

2. Participate politically, and in secular conduits of power, but do so with a determination to "love our enemies, and pray for those who persecute us."

Timothy Keller observes: "In the Good Samaritan parable told in the Gospel of Luke, Jesus points us to a man risking his life to give material help to someone of a different race and religion. Jesus forbids us to withhold help from our neighbors, and this will inevitably require that we participate in political processes. If we experience exclusion and even persecution for doing so, we are assured that God is with us (Matthew 5:10–11) and that some will still see our 'good deeds and glorify God' (1 Peter 2:11–12). If we are only offensive or only attractive to the world and not both, we can be sure we are failing to live as we ought."[32]

To be both offensive and attractive to the world because of our political participation means we are beholden to neither side of the spectrum, but to the way of Jesus alone. And to do that, we worship Jesus above all else, including our chosen party platform. And it means we continually seek Him for the courage to listen to our "enemies" on the other side of the political divide, and risk to love them and even learn from them.

In His hometown synagogue, Jesus stands to read from "the scroll of Isaiah" on Sabbath day. The focal point of this section of Scripture is the mission of the Messiah: "The Spirit of the LORD is upon me, for he has anointed me to bring Good News to the poor. He has sent me to proclaim that captives will be released, that the blind will see, that the oppressed will be set free, and that the time of the LORD's favor has come" (Luke 4:18–19).

Jesus rolls up the scroll, hands it to the synagogue attendant, and sits (rather melodramatically) in "the seat of Moses." Then He proclaims, "The Scripture you've just heard has been fulfilled this very day!" (v. 21). This is shocking to the Sabbath crowd because no one but the coming Messiah is allowed to sit in the seat of Moses—it has been empty for centuries. Jesus intends this to be a defining moment, highlighted by what he *doesn't* read in the scroll. He plants a period where Isaiah had a (functional) comma, excising this: "and with it, the day of God's anger against their enemies."

Jesus is clearly spotlighting a tectonic shift in our focus—He wants us to target "the enemy within us," not the enemy outside us. When we're following the unedited Jesus, we respond to those who see us as enemies (however unfair that seems) with humility, remorse, curiosity, and counter-cultural kindness. We give people a taste of the enemy-loving kingdom of God in the way we interact with them.

---

3. Upend the embedded power narratives in the culture by serving, not flexing.

Dr. Paul Farmer, the legendary infectious disease expert and public health pioneer, lived by a guiding passion he called "The H of G"—it's short for "hermeneutic of generosity."[33] It means he operated from a foundation that assumes the best in others and is determined to help others as a default setting in life. Researchers have explored strategies for undergirding self-worth and identity, comparing two approaches—one inward-looking and one outward-looking. The first approach focuses on promoting our positive qualities and hiding our weaknesses. The second approach focuses on "striving to help others" and "making a positive difference in someone else's life." The H of G was, by far, the more powerful foundation for identity.[34]

People who live out of a secure identity, striving to help others, are conduits for transformation in the world.

To follow the unedited Jesus means we are vulnerable about our weaknesses and take on a posture of serving others rather than muscling our way to the top of the ladder—personally, corporately, or politically. We raise the waterline for life-changing generosity in all our relational environments. Jesus, excoriating the Pharisees for their lifestyle of power-mongering, says: "Everything they do is for show. On their arms they wear extra wide prayer boxes with Scripture verses inside, and they wear robes with extra-long tassels. And they love to sit at the head table at banquets and in the seats of honor in the synagogues. They love to receive respectful greetings as they walk in the marketplaces, and to be called 'Rabbi'" (Matt. 23:5–7).

And later, invited to the home of an important Pharisee for dinner, He witnesses a pathetic competition to land the seats of honor at the head of the table. He urges the power-desperate guests to lower themselves instead, to "take the lowest place at the foot of the table" because "those who exalt themselves will be humbled, and those who humble themselves will be exalted" (Luke 14:10–11).

A church that comingles political power narratives with the gospel of Jesus is driving people away, for good reason.

Practically, this means we're proactively enthusiastic about others' good news and compassionate toward their bad news. We focus on constructive rather than destructive responses to others—look for the lurking beauty in them, even when the ugly seems dominant. We honor others above ourselves. A heart captured by the way of the unedited Jesus wants to give, and in giving it finds wholeness. When psychiatric pioneer Dr. Karl Menninger was asked, "What would you advise a person to do, if that person felt a nervous breakdown coming on?" he said, "Leave your house, find someone in need, and do something to help that person."[35] Serving others not only invests life in them, but also gives us access to the source of that life in ourselves in order to give it. That means the "living water" Jesus has promised us flows through our own soul on its way to splashing onto others.

***

Secular kingdoms advance their mission by decree; Jesus advances the kingdom of God in an upside-down way. A church that comingles political power narratives with the gospel of Jesus is driving people away, for good reason. Though we are tantalized by the political promise of real change, we've seen enough to know those promises are hollow. Writing in *The Atlantic*, Derek Thompson says, "Religion has lost its halo effect in the past three decades, not because science drove God from the public square, but rather because politics did."[36] Celebrated jazz artist Gregory Porter captures the upside-down and inside-out mission of the unedited Jesus in his song "Take Me to the Alley." Here is a Jesus who simply doesn't care about human standards of strength, notoriety, and influence—a Jesus who honors the kingdom of God, not the kingdom of political gain:

> *Well, they guild their houses in preparation for the King*
> *And they line the sidewalks*
> *With every sort of shiny thing*
> *They will be surprised*
> *When they hear him say*
>
> *Take me to the alley*
> *Take me to the afflicted ones*
> *Take me to the lonely ones*
> *That somehow lost their way*
>
> *Let them hear me say*
> *I am your friend*
> *Come to my table*
> *Rest here in my garden*
> *You will have a pardon*[37]

Reflection/Discussion Questions for Individuals or Small Groups

The Comingling
of Kingdoms

- Many have long believed that America is a "Christian nation"—what do you believe, and why?

- What do we lose, and what do we gain, when we tie our national identity to our Christian identity?

- What are examples of the government embracing "the ways of Jesus," and examples of government departing from "the ways of Jesus"?

- If you had to choose, has your worldview more closely aligned with the Church Regnant (the kingdom of God expressed through political power) or the Church Remnant (the kingdom of God expressed through the "divestment of power")? Explain.

- In your life, how have you struggled to trust Jesus with the things that matter most to you? What has helped you to trust Jesus more deeply, and why?

- Jesus refused, over and over, to let others co-opt Him into leading a political revolution—why was He adamant about this? What might have happened had He caved to this pressure?

- What does it mean for you to live as "salt and yeast" in the world, in your everyday life?

- What's something about the way Jesus responds to power, or exercises power, that challenges you? Inspires worship in you?

- In what ways have you struggled to "love your enemies" in this season of your life? In what ways have you reached out to love your enemies?

The Softening of Hard

"I chose you to come out of the world, so it hates you."
JOHN 15:19

I met a middle schooler named Kenyon when I was a twenty-three-year-old counselor at a Christian camp for kids from low-income backgrounds. Many of these young people had never been out of the city before, and most arrived at camp wrestling with deep trauma in their lives. Kenyon's afro was twice the size of his head, a portent for his outsized bravado. His knuckles had scabs and callouses—a subtle clue that he rarely saw a face he didn't want to punch. He was slight, but carried himself like an MMA fighter.

On the second day of camp, I heard shouting on the soccer field and ran over to find Kenyon wailing away on another, much larger, camper. I pulled him, spitting and screaming obscenities, from the crowd of gawkers and dragged him toward the road that led up to the camp—a quarter-mile of dirt and rocks elevated by an eight-percent grade. I told him we were going to walk to the bottom of the hill, then run up it together as discipline for his behavior. I had a tight grip on his arm to emphasize my determination.

But when we rounded a bend to start walking down the hill, he plopped down in the dirt and started sobbing. It took me a moment to get over my shock before I sat down and put my arm around him.

"What's wrong, Kenyon?" I asked gently. I saw big tears starting to carve tracks down his face . . .

Without looking up, he sputtered, "My parents don't love me . . ."

Incredulous, I asked, "Why do you think that?"

"Because," he said, eyes still downcast, "I can do anything, go anywhere, and hang out with anyone I want—I have no rules. I get whatever I want."

The hard edge of my discipline was tapping into deep pain; living a life free of parental boundaries felt like abandonment to Kenyon. In that moment I learned a lesson I've never forgotten . . .

When we sense we can get whatever we want, whenever we want it, for whatever reason we want it, *we feel unloved.*

The human soul craves boundaries, even when we rail against them. When we are well-loved, much is expected of us. When we are poorly loved, nothing is expected of us. We "taste and see" our parents' goodness toward us in the intersection between their passionate tenderness and their passionate expectations. Social scientists call this an "authoritative" parenting style—an approach to identity formation that is proven best for healthy development, and fuels lifelong maturity in kids. "Authoritative parents tend to be demanding and hold high standards of their children, but they also express high levels of warmth and communication with them."[1] Researchers say these phrases characterize this approach to parenting: "I'm the authority here to help you mature" and "Let's talk this out" and "Love holds expectations."[2]

When we are deeply loved, we experience deeply what good is like. Good sacrifices its own comfort to invite us out of our comfort and into something higher and better. Kenyon and I eventually stood up, walked down the hill, then ran up it together. We stood panting at the top. I glanced at his face and could see dignity creeping back into him—the sense that he was someone worthy of expectation.

The hard edges we experience from those who invest their love in us are catalysts for transformation and (outside of abusive behavior) clear evidence that we deeply matter to them. They are focused on the deeper goal of our maturity—and growing into maturity is what goodness feels like. Goodness is not just the way Jesus relates to us; it's His nature. To know Jesus intimately is to be in a continuous cycle of formation, from what our brokenness has done to us into greater and greater wholeness that reflects His glory . . .

Transformation is what Jesus is after in us—He wants a beloved relationship with us, not incremental moral improvements. So, we may imagine a Jesus who is soft to the touch, but He honors our dignity more than we do. And when we dishonor that dignity, or devalue it, His love will feel hard to us. Metaphorically, He "runs the hill" with us.

The Christian-ish Jesus

There is no facet of Jesus more deeply misunderstood, and therefore more widely edited, than the hard-but-good ways He relates to both His enemies and His friends. Because He is good, He is also formidable. Researcher and author Ed Stetzer says: "People like to believe in a generic Christian-ish god with cafeteria doctrines. However, when we ask about harder beliefs—things that the church has and still considers orthodoxy—the numbers shift."[3] So, while almost all Americans (92 percent) believe Jesus was a real human person, about half (52 percent) also believe He sinned during His life on earth. That's because our deep belief is that all human persons are *fallible*, so Jesus is liable to succumb to temptation like all the rest of us. We think of Him as fundamentally soft, not hard, because He's simply one of us fallible people.[4] And so we soften Jesus' hard edges to match our diminished view of Him.

- We think of anger as a sin, but Jesus was often angry, and Paul urged us to "be angry, and yet do not sin" (Eph. 4:26 NASB).
- We think of shrewdness as the manipulative leverage of shysters, but Jesus treated it as a crucial skill that believers must learn to practice (Luke 16:1–9).

- We think of Jesus as "the Prince of Peace," but forget that He told His disciples: "Don't imagine that I came to bring peace to the earth! I came not to bring peace, but a sword" (Matt. 10:34).
- We consider profane speech un-Christian (though we hear plenty of it in our favorite entertainment), but Jesus excoriated the Pharisees, using aggressive and disturbing language (Matt. 23).
- We think of Jesus as affirming people caught up in sin "just as they are," without any expectations of change, but Jesus said to the woman caught in adultery, "Go and sin no more" (John 8:11).

Paul warned his protégé Timothy—and, by extension, us—to watch out for this expectation that the hard truths of Jesus can be softened away: "For a time is coming when people will no longer listen to sound and wholesome teaching. They will follow their own desires and will look for teachers who will tell them whatever their itching ears want to hear. They will reject the [hard] truth and chase after [soft] myths" (2 Tim. 4:3–4).

Scripture offers us so many examples of a Jesus who is hard to swallow that it's remarkable we've managed to recast Him as a bearded, sandal-wearing ray of sunshine. In every page of the gospel accounts of His life, we find Him saying or doing something hard—bitter pills of goodness that seem almost impossible to swallow, including these examples recorded by Matthew:

- **Those who reject the grace of God suffer the consequences.** The message of Jesus' parable of the great feast in Matthew 22 is simple—"Many are called, but few are chosen." In the story, a king prepares an elaborate wedding feast for his son, and sends his servants out to tell the invited guests that everything is ready. But they refuse to come. Perplexed, the king tells his servants to remind the guests that this feast will be like no other they've ever experienced. But the guests ignore the servants, assaulting and even murdering some. The king is furious, and tells his servants to go out into the streets and invite any random people they encounter to the feast. Those who are hungry and eager get to enjoy the king's lavish hospitality—those who take his generosity and grace for granted get nothing. The message: ignore grace at your own peril.

When we're oblivious to the dire consequences of our separation from God, we devalue the impossible gift of His grace. If we have fallen onto a train track, unaware of the approaching locomotive, it's best to grab the hand that is reaching down to pull us to safety, not spit on it.

- **Those who marry and later divorce may have good reasons for splitting, but they are tearing apart something God has "joined together."** A conniving group of Pharisees, intent on trapping Jesus into saying something that will get Him in trouble, asks Him: "Should a man be allowed to divorce his wife for just any reason?" Jesus responds with an edge—divorce is not okay for *just any reason*: "Since they are no longer two but one, let no one split apart what God has joined together." The Pharisees see an opening, so they ask Jesus why Moses allowed for divorce. And Jesus is blunt: "[It's] a concession to your hard hearts, but it was not what God had originally intended. And I tell you this, whoever divorces his wife and marries someone else commits adultery—unless his wife has been unfaithful" (Matt. 19:8–9).

  Men who divorce their wives for *just any reason*, He says, "commit adultery." Here He is firing a shot across the bow at men who hold all the control in their marriage relationship, often abusing that power by casting aside their wives indiscriminately. Among these powerful religious leaders are many who have used Moses' "divorce permission" to trade in their wives for a new model whenever they feel like it. These divorced women receive no "divorce decree," so they can never marry again, and are dependent on others for survival. Here Jesus is not addressing divorce so much as He is addressing the power dynamics between couples at that time. Women were treated as "less than" men—Jesus is disgusted by those who propagate this demeaning and brutalizing patriarchal system, and He is calling them out for it.

- **Jesus is called "family friendly," but He does not sow peace in families.** In His instructions to His disciples before they head out on the road to "heal the sick, raise the dead, cure those with leprosy, and cast out demons," Jesus reorders their cultural understanding of the primacy of family. In Jewish culture, no obedience is higher than the obedience you owe your parents, especially your father. But Jesus says: "Don't imagine that I came to bring peace to the earth! I came not to bring peace, but a sword." Quoting the prophet Micah, He rails on: "'I have come to set a man against his father, a daughter against her mother.'... If you love your father or mother more than you love me, you are not worthy of being mine" (Matt. 10:34–37).

  Jesus isn't coming to bring peace, because Jesus is the Truth. Though we assume truth is unifying, it's actually the opposite. Truth creates division because it is often hard to accept, and forces us to decide where we stand. David Foster Wallace reminds us: "The truth will set you free. But not before it's done with you."[5] Jesus did not come to appease, but to transform. And, by definition, transformation is a reordering of what existed before. We lose what we have to gain what we don't have.

- **Jesus has little patience for those who have heard and seen Him do remarkable things, but still don't believe.** When a desperate man brings his demon-possessed boy to Jesus for healing, he laments that His disciples couldn't do the job. "You faithless and corrupt people!" He blusters. "How long must I be with you? How long must I put up with you? Bring the boy here to me" (Matt. 17:17). And Jesus promptly rebukes the demon inside the boy, releasing him from bondage. We expect a Jesus who is long-suffering with us, who shrugs off our disbelief in the face of His repeated displays of authority and power. It's jolting to hear "faithless and corrupt," but a jolt is (sometimes) exactly what we need.

The Good Purpose of Pruning

Jesus is tender and kind and forgiving—shockingly so. And these stories, and so many more, remind us that He's also what we might call an "in your face" person. That's because He is the definition of goodness, and goodness is determined to promote growth in us—all growing things have "abundant life," and all withering things are sliding into decay and (later) death. This is why we see His goodness, sometimes, only in retrospect. The tree that has its branches pruned cannot see goodness in it, but when that tree is thriving and full of abundant fruit, it recognizes the good heart behind the hand that gripped the shears. The goodness in Jesus intends to bring abundant life into our lives—so abundant that it bubbles over in us and splashes onto others. And this abundance of goodness is a result of growth, not riches or satisfaction or even happiness.

New York Times op-ed columnist David Brooks, in his essay "Five Lies Our Culture Tells," says one of the five is *I can make myself happy*: "This is the lie of self-sufficiency. This is the lie that happiness is an individual accomplishment. If I can have just one more victory, lose 15 pounds or get better at meditation, then I will be happy. But people looking back on their lives from their deathbeds tell us that happiness is found amid thick and loving relationships. It is found by defeating self-sufficiency for a state of mutual dependence. It is found in the giving and receiving of care."[6] In our sheepy self-narratives, we can't stop believing the lie that self-sufficiency will lead to happiness—the deepest form of assumed goodness. But real goodness is found in "mutual dependency." That's true in our human relationships, but profoundly true in our relationship with Jesus. It's our dependence that opens us to pruning—another way of describing "the giving and receiving of care."

I graduated college with two journalism degrees—as a senior, I had to take a Public-Affairs Reporting class taught by the department's toughest professor. We had to find a publisher for all our reporting assignments. I had a leg up because I was an editor for the university newspaper. The journalism department chair read one of the lengthy investigative pieces I'd published for the class and told me he wanted to enter it in a prestigious national student journalism competition. On the same day I learned that my piece won third place among all college journalists, my professor handed back our graded articles. I got a C-minus on that award-winner . . .

Now that's setting the bar high. But that professor had his eye on my long-term success as a journalist, not on short-term satisfaction with impressive writing that camouflaged obvious flaws. He cared for me— enough to give me a C-minus and stick by it even when other students challenged him in light of the national award my article had won. In that moment, I did not experience this professor's hard input as good—exactly the opposite, actually.

But this one act of "pruning," now more than forty years ago, has translated to an explosion of fruit from my "branches," marking both my working life and personal life with joy. His C-minus cut into my lazy disregard for the whole truth, and generated a lifelong hunger for the beauty of transcendent truth. This is the fruitfulness that creates deeper beauty—a beauty that others can "taste and see" as goodness. And it is not possible without the hard edge of elevated expectation. No pruning = diminished beauty = diminished goodness.

Mis-describing Jesus

We have a love/hate relationship with hardship. We want things to be easier than they are, but we also know that we grow the most under the duress of great challenges.

Because of our discomfort with the engines of growth, and our entitled posture toward enjoying the good fruits of growth outside of the personal cost of it, we don't know what to do with the hard edges of Jesus. The Jesus of the Bible is not the Jesus we want or expect or assume, because He is more interested in our growth than our (short-term) happiness. And so we edit Him to fit what is tolerable to us in the moment.

When my oldest daughter was in middle school, I often chauffeured her friends to church activities. In one of those ten-minute car rides, a girl who'd just served as a leader in a churchwide worship experience was excitedly describing it to my daughter. She'd spent several days serving on a ministry team, introducing people to a deeper relationship with Jesus through a carefully planned encounter. Her passion for what she'd just participated in was contagious. So I told her I was in the middle of a research project, asking people all over the country to simply describe Jesus. "Would you mind telling me some words you'd use to describe Jesus to someone who's never heard of Him?" I asked. I could see her scrunched forehead in the rearview mirror—she was thinking long and hard about it. Finally, cautiously, she offered this: "Well, I'd have to say He's really, really nice."

I waited to see if she was going to add more "texture" to that response, but she seemed happy with it. So I asked a follow-up question: "Remember that time Jesus made a whip and chased all the moneychangers out of the temple? How does that story fit with the way you describe Jesus?" The girl's forehead scrunched again, and the car descended into awkward silence. Finally, exasperated, the girl found an escape route: "Well, I know Jesus is nice, so what He did must have been nice."

Because this girl was so young, it would be easy to discount her response—except it's not all that different from the prevailing way *most* people, not just middle schoolers, think about Jesus. In that countrywide research project I referenced, I hired videographers in five cities to stop people on the street and ask them to describe Jesus using the first words that came to mind. The dominant word was always "nice." But there's an easier way to get at this question—just plug "descriptive words about Jesus" into Google and see what pops up. These are the top responses: loving, peaceful, forgiving, peacemaker, meek, forgiving, revitalizing, pure, gentle, and humble. *In other words, "nice."*

Yes, Jesus was conventionally nice when He offered marginalized people dignity, or when He healed their physical ailments or (especially!) when He raised them from the dead. But to confine His behavior to the boundaries of "nice," we have to edit out the countless times He blasted religious leaders ("whitewashed tombs," "total frauds," and "snakes"). And we have to overlook the number of times He called His followers foolish, or set the bar so high that many stopped following Him altogether because they were offended or overwhelmed. And we have to re-explain or overlook His apparent rudeness to people who hosted Him in their home

(Martha in Luke 10 and a religious law expert in Luke 11, for example). And we have to redact the upended way almost everyone, everywhere reacted when they encountered Him.

Boston College professor and C. S. Lewis scholar Peter Kreeft says it well: "I think Jesus is the only man in history who never bored anyone. I think this an empirical fact, not just a truth of faith. . . . Not everyone who meets Jesus is pleased, and not everyone is happy. But everyone is shocked."[7] His disruptive behavior and His polarizing rhetoric are a blaring intrusion into our visions of a Jesus who is more like Mr. Rogers than a "Skandalon" or "Lion of the Tribe of Judah." But the hard edges of Jesus remind us that He is deeply good, and has come to remake us in His image, not rubber-stamp our default inclinations to live as if we are our own gods. This is the goodness of a parent (or even a pet owner) who can see what we don't see.

Cats usually clean themselves with determined expertise, but we had a cat named Penny who did not. She desperately needed a bath, but in a cat's reality, the tub might as well be a woodchipper. I had to manhandle her into the water while my wife desperately scrubbed her hinterlands. It was all for her good, but try telling that to a spitting, clawing, oversoaked cat. I'd violated her trust. For weeks she avoided me. If she only understood the goodness on the other side of this terrible experience, she might grow to appreciate the fruits of it—the stored-up treasure of joy, rescued from her own squalor. In the meantime, she would have to trust in my good heart toward her, across the chasm of an experience that seemed to prove the opposite.

The Exclusionary Jesus

This Jesus—the upending, upsetting Jesus—is contrary to our mental maps of who we expect Him to be. *This Jesus* says and does things that most of us who go to church or say we believe in Him tacitly ignore or discount. And often, it's *this Jesus* that the progressive or liberal end of the church surgically edits because He appears to violate the primacy of compassion. In an exploration of the shared faith of the Christian right and left, writer Ruth Terry says: "While conservative evangelicalism tends to focus on sin, repentance, and salvation, the Christian Left identify Christ's radical love and inclusion for marginalized people as the locus of their faith."[8] When we elevate *inclusion*, making it the superseding mission of Jesus on earth, we inevitably edit out His many, many *hard boundaries and exclusions.* Here are two examples from one chapter in the gospel of Matthew:

JESUS SAYS: "You can enter God's Kingdom only through the narrow gate. The highway to hell is broad, and its gate is wide for the many who choose that way. But the gateway to life is very narrow and the road is difficult, and only a few ever find it" (Matt. 7:13–14).

BUT MANY OF US SAY: "The gate into heaven is wide." Six out of ten American Christians (58 percent) say people from other religions will enter heaven, not hell, at the end of their life. Two-thirds of Americans (67 percent) say most people are basically good, and good people will go to heaven—doing good things, or doing things in God's name, ensures "peace with God."[9] Very few (18 percent) of us believe that "small sins" will lead to a thumbs-down on judgment day. Put another way, conventional thinking about hell among Christians flips Jesus' declaration into something like this: *The highway to hell is narrow, and the gate to get in is tiny for the few who unwittingly stumble through it.*

My college-age daughter texted me late one night to ask about the "hard" reality of hell—she was locked in a debate with a close friend who'd read a book that questions how a loving God could "condemn" people to an eternity of torture. Nothing about the doctrine of hell seems "soft."

And yet, the Jesus who *embodies* love and goodness talks about it all the time. Writing for The Gospel Coalition, Leslie Schmucker observes: "Jesus doesn't only reference hell, he describes it in great detail. He says it is a place of eternal torment (Luke 16:23), of unquenchable fire (Mark 9:43), where the worm does not die (Mark 9:48), where people will gnash their teeth in anguish and regret (Matt. 13:42), and from which there is no return, even to warn loved ones (Luke 16:19–31). He calls hell a place of 'outer darkness' (Matt. 25:30), comparing it to 'Gehenna' (Matt. 10:28), which was a trash dump outside the walls of Jerusalem where rubbish was burned and maggots abounded. . . . There's no denying that Jesus knew, believed, and warned about the absolute reality of hell."[10]

The hard edge of a Jesus who talks openly of hell is an irritant to our tidy definitions of love. But a love that disregards human agency, overwhelming it by making our choice to submit (or not) to God's grace a certainty, violates the "truly free" life Jesus is inviting us into (John 8:36). Satan "kills, steals, and destroys" by obliterating human agency; Jesus invites us into "abundant life" by dignifying human agency. In response to my daughter's question about hell, I texted back:

> Well, hell is a place, but not in the way we think of "place"—as if it was a geographical location. Hell is a place in the same way that heaven is a place. I don't believe heaven is really a "mansion with many rooms," but that's the metaphor Jesus uses for it. Like all His metaphors, He's using something we understand to help us comprehend something that's hard for us to understand—how things really are in the Kingdom of God. So, hell is real because Jesus said it is; a relational separation from God that is the result of our choice, not His choice. . . . This is the truth that C. S. Lewis so beautifully weaves into his book The Great Divorce. Read the story Jesus told about Lazarus and the Rich Man in Luke 16. People have their own agency, and God won't violate it. If they reject Jesus here, they'll reject Him there. To follow Jesus means that He always has the last word; that means no theology of hell that plainly contradicts Jesus's teaching on it is true.

The hardness of Jesus' love only seems hard in comparison to our empty versions of it.

Eternal separation from God as a "punishment" for not trusting in His salvation seems, on the face of it, unloving. But it is a deeper violation of love to imagine away our choice to trust, or not to trust, Jesus. When we do, we diminish our image-bearing dignity, lowering ourselves to God's house pets, not His beloveds. The hardness of Jesus' love only seems hard in comparison to our empty versions of it.

JESUS SAYS: **"But anyone who hears my teaching and doesn't obey it is foolish, like a person who builds a house on sand.** When the rains and floods come and the winds beat against that house, it will collapse with a mighty crash" (Matt. 7:26–27).

BUT MANY OF US SAY: **"I can construct 'the foundation of my house' using beliefs mined from a mash-up of faith traditions."** Half of Americans (45 percent) say the Bible "is written for each person to interpret as they choose."[11] And Notre Dame sociologist Dr. Christian Smith adds: "No more than 15 percent of the total emerging adult population embrace a strong religious faith. Thirty percent tend to customize their faith to fit the rest of their lives."[12] The majority of us base our beliefs, and our expectations of eternal life, on a foundation constructed from the "sand" of many faiths.[13]

It's impossible to reconcile the exclusionary Jesus—"I am the way, the truth, and the life; no one can come to the Father except through me" (John 14:6)—with the softened, inclusionary Jesus who will look the other way when we embrace beliefs that directly contradict His emphatic orthodoxies. Biblically, to follow Jesus means to submit to Him as our Rabbi—we are His *talmids*, or apprentices. The "narrow way" He calls us to is not a reference to people who are judged worthy to enter the kingdom of heaven. Instead, it's about a "narrowing" of options for how we seek formation as people. To follow the unedited Jesus means to lay down other ways of life so that we can pursue a specific way of life taught and modeled by Him, our "true Rabbi."

Walking the Way of (the Unedited) Jesus

What will it look like if we walk in the way of the unedited Jesus, refusing to soften His hard edges and embracing the whole menu of His love for us? It will mean that we grow more and more comfortable living in *tension*. Jesus invites us to live in the tension between two competing cultures—the Kingdom of God (His "native country") and the Kingdom of Broken Humanity. When we follow Him, we enter into this tension—where the values/customs/truths of one kingdom are at odds with the values/customs/truths of the other. Jesus prays: "I'm not asking you to take them out of the world, but to keep them safe from the evil one. They do not belong to this world any more than I do. . . . Just as you sent me into the world, I am sending them into the world" (John 17:15–18). We are sent into the world but must remain "unbelonging" in the world—this tension is the true cost of our discipleship.

The best way to embrace two-kingdom tension is to test our apprecentice-submission—we survey our taken-for-granted beliefs and practices, then assess them in light of the habits, teachings, and priorities of our Rabbi. These questions will help:

1. What does Jesus actually say and do in the gospel accounts of His life?

If we simply slow down and list everything Jesus said and did in the gospels, breaking it all down into categories (such as "challenging," "hard," "scandalous," "generous," "evasive," "effusive," "tender," "passionate," or "brave"), we'll discover a Jesus who shatters our common misconceptions.

So try this very exercise—limit it to a chapter in one of the Gospels, for starters. Then look at your list and ask yourself a hard question: "Is this the Jesus I'm following and serving?" Keep at it until an internal "switch" is turned on, when questioning the "givens" in your beliefs and practices becomes like breathing for you. Decide if you will live your life as a talmid—a follower of Jesus—or stay in the safe confines of the pick-and-choose crowd. To follow Jesus means to stop propagating the myth of Him as merely "nice" and start worshiping the unedited Jesus, who is so much bigger and better than our reductionist versions that we can't help but worship Him.

2. Am I living by the "Good-Person Points System," or am I inviting Jesus to define goodness for me?

In the groundbreaking Michael Schur series *The Good Place* (a comedy that aims to tackle theological tensions and poke holes in our "good person" belief system), an angel tells a crowd of heaven's new arrivals that they've made it to "the Good Place," and explains the complex "Points System" that made it possible:

Welcome to your first day in the afterlife. You were all, simply put, good people. But how do we know that you were good? . . . During your time on Earth, every one of your actions had a positive or a negative value, depending on how much good or bad that action put into the universe. . . . Every single thing you did had an effect that rippled out over time and ultimately created some amount of good or bad. . . . When your time on Earth has ended, we calculate the total value of your life using our perfectly accurate measuring system. Only the people with the very highest scores, the true cream of the crop, get to come here, to the Good Place.[14]

Much later in the show, we find out that the Points System is actually created in hell, not heaven. The angel describing the system is actually a demon. Assigning points to good and bad behavior sounds fair, but it's more like torture. When are good deeds good enough? Who gets to decide what's good and what's not? What happens when I (inevitably) do bad things? Are my strongly held beliefs about goodness consistent with the words and actions of Jesus?

When a brash young man approaches Jesus to show off his "high score" in the Good-Person Points System, he first addresses Him as "Good Teacher." Jesus responds slyly: "Why do you call me good? Only God is truly good" (Luke 18:18–23). It's our intimate attachment to goodness, not our false attainment of its counterfeits, that frees us from the broader culture's definitions of what is good and what is not. When we follow Jesus, our practice of goodness transcends political parties, family traditions, cultural expectations, and pragmatism. Our love for others looks sometimes soft and sometimes hard.

---

3. The whole of the law is summed up simply—love God, and love your neighbor—but what does love require, and who is my neighbor?

A reporter from *Politico* asked Serene Jones: "The Bible exhorts us to 'love thy neighbor as thyself.' Does the divide between the Christian right and left boil down to, in part, a disagreement over who my 'neighbor' is and what 'love' means? And in that context, do you see 'love' as political?" Jones responded: "Absolutely, I see love as political. All the people who say, 'love thy neighbor as thyself,' and who say that as a truth, need to think deeply about what that means. Can you love your neighbor as yourself and refuse to feed them, or put them in cages or deny them basic health care? Is that love? . . . Loving your neighbor and believing in fundamental equality are not moral givens in the political actions of people, and that's the step we need to take."[15]

Jones is pointing out a vital truth—we must slow down when we're answering the "What is love? Who is our neighbor?" questions and consider how Jesus answers them, then decide if we are following Jesus or following the edited version of Him that fits our preconceived priorities. But the ways in which Jesus practices "loving our neighbors" would offend people on both ends of the theological spectrum. Author and editor Drew Dyck says: "I'm convinced that if Jesus was doing his earthly ministry today, he'd run afoul of both liberals and conservatives. He'd scandalize liberals with exclusive truth claims and inflexible sexual ethics. Meanwhile he'd rankle conservatives by undermining their authority or telling parables of 'the Good Muslim.' He'd tell someone to empty their 401k and give the money to the poor. In the end both sides would be saying the same thing as Jesus' contemporaries: let's get rid of this guy."[16]

The prompt for Jesus' parable of the good Samaritan (Luke 10:25–37) is a Pharisee who asks, "What should I do to inherit eternal life?" Jesus asks him to answer instead, and the man responds, "Love God, love your neighbors." But then he wants to know who he's required to love and who he can ignore. So Jesus tells him a story about a man beaten by thieves, lying by the side of the road. The Pharisee knows Jesus is going to insert him as a character in this story—that's the point of His parable-response. But he's not the first passerby (a Sadducee), not the second passerby (a Levite), and not even the third passerby—a man who doesn't even belong in the story, a Samaritan. London School of Theology professor Conrad Gempf says, "It's like Jesus is telling a story about the Civil War, and a guy in a space suit floats in."[17] Jesus makes the neighbor-loving Samaritan the impossible hero of the story, so the beaten and needy person he helps (the only "unassigned" character) must be the Pharisee who asked Jesus, "Who is my neighbor?"

The victimized and helpless man who receives help from a low-life Samaritan is, in real life, the same one who would never return the favor. To the Pharisees, Samaritans don't qualify as "neighbors"—they're barely human. Jesus is calling them out for their arrogance and self-righteousness. And He's suggesting their hope for "inheriting eternal life" hinges on a renovated understanding of who is worthy of love. *What if you are not the hero of this story, or even a disinterested passerby—what if you are the one in need of love from the very people you denigrate?*

Jesus upends all our assumptions about what love is, and who we're to extend that love to. He is setting the standard for how, and to whom, our love is expressed. We "ask, seek, and knock" in our relationship with Him, continually turning to Him for guidance, because we elevate His "standards and practices" above our own. Following Him means we ingest those standards and practices as we love Him, and as we love others. Because He gets the final word, our love sometimes feels transformationally soft to others, and sometimes transformationally hard.

We can see this repeatedly modeled by Jesus—He offers soft love to the marginalized, the victimized, and the needy; He offers hard love to the arrogant, the bullying, and the ignorant. Both kinds of love have redemptive intent. But that intent is expressed differently, according to the needs of the person. Jesus is an artist, and He intends to use the raw material of our life to re-form us—that's what "born again" really means. *Your hard edges are hard to accept,* said the clay to the Potter.

Reflection/Discussion Questions for Individuals or Small Groups
The Softening of Hard

- How have others' expectations of you communicated love? How have others' expectations of you been harmful instead? What's the difference between expectations that harm and those that love?

- Growing up, how closely did your parents reflect an "authoritative" parenting style? Explain.

- How do you see the "good" in the hard ways Jesus sometimes relates to others? How have you seen the "hard edges" of Jesus bring goodness in your life?

- What's something "exclusionary" about Jesus that is hard for you, and why? We can usually explain why inclusion is a good thing, but why is exclusion a good thing?

- What's a "common misconception" you've had about Jesus, and how has it been challenged?

- In what ways have you lived by the "Good Person Points System" in your life, and what impact has that had?

- In what ways is "loving your neighbor" a "soft" thing? In what ways is it a "hard" thing?

3

The Marginalization of the Poor

✳ ✳ ✳

**"God blesses those who are poor . . .
for the Kingdom of Heaven is theirs."**

MATTHEW 5:3

Let's revisit a story from chapter 2, an encounter Jesus has with an extraordinary young man.

He's that guy you knew in high school—valedictorian, GPA padded north of 4.0, captain of the debate team, and varsity tennis player. He's headed to the Ivy League. In youth group at church, his hand was always up, and his answers were always right. After college, he lands a full-ride at an elite law school. And after that, he's recruited for a plum job at a prestigious firm, where he's soon asked to join as a partner. It's this young man, the "rich young ruler," who runs up to Jesus and kneels before Him, just before He departs for Jerusalem and Golgotha.

"Good Teacher," he says, "what must I do to inherit eternal life?" And Jesus (likely less stern than we imagine) responds: "Why do you call me good? Only God is truly good." And then He lists the conventional requirements for "goodness." But the man, so earnest that Jesus feels "genuine love" for him, replies: "I've obeyed all these commandments since I was young." Jesus is full of empathy for the man, but is determined to roll a spiritual grenade his way: "There is still one thing you haven't done. Go and sell all your possessions and give the money to the poor, and you will have treasure in heaven. Then come, follow me."

We know what happens next—the crestfallen and confused young man slinks away. Of the many lessons we have extracted from this awkward encounter in Mark 10, here is one we likely have not heard from a church pulpit:

Jesus advocates the transfer of wealth from a godly, hard-working, and industrious religious leader to the poor and disenfranchised.

It's a request that smacks of left-wing socialism, except for who said it. The American success narrative recasts Jesus as a capitalist, not an advocate for redistributing wealth. But when Jesus asks the man to do this, He's intentionally undermining the misguided belief system of those who believe (as was common in ancient Jewish culture) that wealth is a sign of God's favor. In old covenant culture, conventional wisdom asserts the poor are poor *for a reason*—that God sorts the good from the bad using the gold standard. But beyond the man's religious obedience ("I've obeyed all these commandments since I was young"), Jesus wants the man to know that the path of righteousness always leads into the heart of God, where a fierce advocacy for the poor burns at the core.

It is not a stretch to say that if Jesus appeared incognito today, advocating a similar value system, He would be vilified in much of the church.

His disciples, shocked by the ramifications of what Jesus has done, protest: "Then who in the world can be saved?" And Jesus responds by patiently explaining that God is looking for people who will offer themselves as conduits for blessing the poor with tangible help—offering resources, compassion, and presence that will help lift them out of their rutted degradation and give them the opportunity to live in dignity.

It is not a stretch to say that if Jesus appeared incognito today, advocating a similar value system, He would be vilified in much of the church. The belief that the rich deserve their spoils just as much as the poor deserve their neediness means that we treat the "have-nots" with suspicion—the forces that have led to their poverty are often assumed to be character-driven, the same "summary verdict" embraced in the time of Jesus. *If you invest the effort, as I have, to create a prosperous life, you'll reap the rewards—you don't have, because you don't try. God doesn't bless slackers.*

The pecking order that grew up under the misinterpretations of the "law and the prophets" dictated that a person's life condition was a result of sin, obvious or hidden. Likewise, though we live under a new covenant inaugurated by Jesus, many of us have embraced the debunked value system of the Old Testament meritocracy. We have ignored or edited the words and actions of Jesus, whose tenderness toward the poor was fueled by His admiration for their courage and a fierce sensitivity to their neediness. If we use the early church as a model for how to live in community and spread the good news of Jesus to the world, those believers, directly influenced by the teachings of Jesus, fed thousands of poor people every day in the Roman Empire during the rule of Emperor Julian.[1] They cared for the "outsiders," not just fellow Jews. And these Christians who dedicated themselves to serving the poor transformed Roman culture.

What Jesus Hates and Loves

In the church, we try to pay attention to what Jesus honored and embraced. But we can also learn deep truths about the heart of Jesus if we pay attention to what disgusts Him. On the heels of another rough debate with the privileged and conniving Pharisees ("Everything they do is for show"), He turns to the crowd and lowers the boom. He's targeting traits in these religious leaders (and the culture they promote) He just can't stand—many of them tied to their relationship with the poor.

- They are so enamored of wealth that they swear by it as if it was their god, rather than release it to serve those who need it (Matt. 23:16–19).
- They are careful to tithe their income while simultaneously withholding economic mercy from those who need it (Matt. 23:23).

- They have clothed themselves with greed and self-indulgence in the presence of those who struggle to clothe themselves with the basics of survival (Matt. 23:25).

Even though these scathing critiques are lobbed at a strata of the population that seems beneath us (*we are not hypocritical posers like the Pharisees*), they could just as easily describe prevalent attitudes in the church. In the US, 247 million people identify as Christian, but only 1.5 million (.6 percent) tithe.[2] Christians who *do* give spend 2.5 percent of their income to help the poor—compare that to Depression-era Christians who gave 3 percent. Households making over $75,000 are the least charitable.[3] One more eye-opener—in a Barna survey of Americans, conservative evangelicals over the age of twenty-five were least likely to list "serving the poor" as an important contribution of the church.[4] In contrast, those eighteen to twenty-nine list "serv[ing] the poor through my church" as a major reason they've stayed committed to churchgoing when so many of their peers have dropped out.[5]

In making his startling case that the greatest gift of God to His people is Jesus Himself, not the salvation He offers us, Andrew Wilson (teaching pastor at King's Church London) highlights the Messiah's determination to give with generous abandon to those who need it:

> Many parables in the Gospels present God as an irrepressible giver, even when the parable has other goals. Once there was a farmer who scattered seed so liberally that most of it didn't take root. Once there was a king who forgave a debt of 10,000 talents (millions of dollars today). Once there was a vineyard owner who gave people far more than their work was worth. Once there was a father who gave away half his estate to his rebellious son—and then gave him a feast when he came crawling back, having wasted it all. Once there was a nobleman who gave three months' wages to all his employees, and then went on a foreign trip. Once there was a landowner who gave his vineyard over to tenants. Once there was a king who gave wedding invitations to every undesirable in the county.[6]

Generosity characterizes Jesus' default response to every need He meets. He is perpetually upending the world's value system, elevating the poor and overturning the rich. In His first sermon, the first words out of Jesus' mouth are: "God blesses those who are poor and realize their need for him, for the Kingdom of Heaven is theirs" (Matt. 5:3). The poor are blessed because they are the rightful heirs to the kingdom of heaven, where trusting dependence on God is the norm. Jesus is saying that the poor are already experiencing the culture and value system that characterizes the life of the Trinity. They are "blessed" when their struggles make them viscerally aware of their need for His love and provision, and discover they are beloved: "Are two sparrows not sold for an assarion [a copper coin]? And yet not one of them will fall to the ground apart from your Father" (Matt. 10:29 NASB). When what we lack makes us awake to His care for us, we understand goodness the way children do—that precious treasures are wrapped in relationship, and the "good life" transcends what can be monetized.

Life is really about which kingdom we will choose to live in—the kingdom of secularism (*the kingdom in which we are kings*) or the kingdom of God. When we have abundant resources, we have no innate motivation to pursue resources outside ourselves. To be rich is to be poor, in that the affluent are able to draw from their own resources and more likely to avoid a visceral dependence on God, and so end up relationally deprived. To be poor is to be rich, in that the impoverished are more likely prompted to draw from resources in the heart of God and end up invited into the richness of His presence.

In his essay "A World Without Jesus?" writer and pastor Larry Lasiter observes: "Before the teachings of Jesus influenced the cultures of the world, it was believed RIGHT that the strong should dominate the weak, the young dominate the old, the rich have favor over the poor and men treat women and children as property."[7] This value system is repugnant when it is condensed into a sentence, but when it is dispersed into the world it is often undetectable, creeping into every aspect of our life. We ingest it the same way we ingest pollutants in the air that we can't see or smell.

In his iconic keynote address at the 2006 National Prayer Breakfast, U2 frontman and social activist Bono exposed the bad air we're all breathing, and reminded the rich and powerful that God's kingdom welcomes the poor:

> Look, whatever thoughts you have about God . . . most will agree that if there is a God, He has a special place for the poor. In fact, the poor are where God lives . . . I mean, God may well be with us in our mansions on the hill . . . I hope so . . . But the one thing we can all agree, all faiths and ideologies, is that God is with the vulnerable and poor. God is in the slums, in the cardboard boxes where the poor play house . . . God is in the silence of a mother who has infected her child with a virus that will end both their lives . . . God is in the cries heard under the rubble of war . . . God is in the debris of wasted opportunity and lives, and God is with us if we are with them.[8]

Our Relationship with Neediness

Our posture toward the poor is central to the culture of the kingdom of God. It is a primary way we reflect the heart of God, not a P.S. expressed by our end-of-year giving. It's not simply a question of compassion or empathy—it's a clear reflection of our embedded value system and our assumptions about who Jesus is and what He honors. It's the "realization of need" that He highlights in the poor, the doorway into His presence.

After the rich young man slinks away, disappointed and discouraged, Jesus tells His disciples: "I tell you the truth, it is very hard for a rich person to enter the Kingdom of Heaven. I'll say it again—it is easier for a camel to go through the eye of a needle than for a rich person to enter the Kingdom of God!" Like us, His disciples are dumbfounded by this contradiction of conventional wisdom. And sly Jesus looks at them "intently" and responds: "Humanly speaking it is impossible [for the rich to find their way into the Kingdom of God]. But with God everything is possible" (Matt. 19:23–26). Even the rich have hope of entering the kingdom, He's saying, but they have hope only through their dependence on Jesus, not because of anything they have achieved.

Jesus is pointing out that our visceral experience of neediness will define our relationship with God. The poor are needy by definition, and that neediness naturally propels them toward dependence. Yes, dependence can lead to desperate acts of self-reliance and degradation, but it is also a primary on-ramp into intimacy in our relationship with Jesus. In fact, all of the people who migrated inside Jesus' circle of close relationships were needy and dependent. They moved beyond a belief in their own god-ness by acknowledging and embracing their desperation—"I need more than what I have; I need God." The people who seemed to "get" this also gravitated toward Jesus. That's because those who see themselves as fundamentally needy also see the unedited Jesus as He really is.

"The Kingdom of God belongs to those who are like children" (Matt. 19:14), and children in the time of Jesus were seen as "fearful, weak, helpless, fragile, dependent, defenseless, and vulnerable."[9] These are the very words that material wealth is supposed to hold at bay—the rich (and those who aspire to be rich) are seeking assurance that none of these words will ever apply to them. And because their affluence allows them to construct a façade that makes them appear less needy than the poor, the rich naturally elevate their worth above them.

It's not possible for us to elevate ourselves above neediness and also hunger and thirst for Jesus—He will have to enter into our satiated false-reality through the back door. That is, through the emotional distress the affluent feel when they "have it all," but discover it isn't enough. Arizona State psychology professor Suniya Luthar studies resilience in teenagers, and her work reveals that affluent kids are among the most emotionally distressed in America. "These kids are incredibly anxious and perfectionistic," she says, but there's "contempt and scorn for the idea that kids who have it all might be hurting."[10] It's through this back door of emotional pain that the rich experience neediness, making it "possible to enter the Kingdom of God."

In this kingdom, the poor experience a kind of countercultural privilege and the rich experience a more subtle form of suffering, in contrast to what Peter Berger calls our Western plausibility structures. David Brooks explains:

[We believe the lie that] rich and successful people are worth more than poorer and less successful people. We pretend we don't tell this lie, but our whole meritocracy points to it. In fact, the meritocracy contains a skein of lies. The message of the meritocracy is that you are what you accomplish. The false promise of the meritocracy is that you can earn dignity by attaching yourself to prestigious brands. The emotion of the meritocracy is conditional love—that if you perform well, people will love you. The sociology of the meritocracy is that society is organized around a set of inner rings with the high achievers inside and everyone else further out. The anthropology of the meritocracy is that you are not a soul to be saved but a set of skills to be maximized.[11]

Walking the Way of (the Unedited) Jesus

What will it look like if we walk in the way of the unedited Jesus, moving our relationship with the poor from the margins of our life to the center? Because we subtly, and not-so-subtly, create Jesus in our own image, we assume Jesus agrees with our cultural lies about poverty. Our way forward is to shatter the Jesus that we've made in our own image and re-embrace the Jesus revealed by Scripture. We stop compartmentalizing Him based on our surface understandings of what He is for and against. We stop propagating a Jesus who doesn't really exist and start advancing His mission, values, and priorities on earth—we become emissaries from a beautiful, foreign land called the kingdom of God. For starters, we might try something from this menu of possibilities:

---

1. Give resources to the poor, and support systemic changes that will uplift them.

Some point to Jesus declaring "The poor you will always have with you" as evidence that poverty is simply an inevitable reality that we should all learn to accept. But this is not what Jesus meant. He's quoting Deuteronomy 15:11, but the context is clear—because of our greed and unwillingness to sacrifice on behalf of the poor, the poor will always be with us. Speaking through Moses, God tells His people: "That is why I am commanding you to share freely with the poor" (Deut. 15:11b).

When we repent of our disinterested and dismissive attitude toward poverty and lean into it instead, we resist the gravitational pull toward greed—we follow Jesus by adopting His habits of generosity, Dr. Paul Farmer's "the H of G." As we "give what we have to give" to the poor, trusting Jesus to guide our generosity, we invest our trust in His promise: "Look at the birds of the sky, that they do not sow, nor reap, nor gather crops into barns, and yet your heavenly Father feeds them. Are you not much more important than they?" (Matt. 6:26 NASB). In our care for the poor, we remind Jesus that we see and appreciate what matters to Him, even when it costs us.

> **When we repent of our disinterested and dismissive attitude toward poverty and lean into it instead, we resist the gravitational pull toward greed.**

When possible, give through relationally connected conduits. Millions of people around the world support children living in poverty through the Christian aid organizations Compassion and World Vision—since college, my wife and I have been among them. Our monthly giving directly resources the everyday needs and education of two children, one in Ecuador and one in Zambia. Even more, we are connected to these children relationally. Through letters and pictures we've watched two of these kids (our first matches) grow from childhood to independent adulthood. These organizations know that a relational connection to giving has a much better shot at turning into a lifelong commitment. Our giving to the poor is now tied to relationships we care about—we are invested in more ways than financially. Give, and whenever possible, give relationally.

Find your excess and give it away. Garage sales are among the most incongruous of American traditions. In the most affluent culture in the history of the world, we collect our excess resources and spend the better part of a weekend selling them for pennies on the dollar. Meanwhile, the poor, whose lives could be transformed by the clothes and furniture and household appliances and tools and art we no longer want or need, go without.

Early on in our marriage, Bev had a growing conviction about our excess resources—under her direction and passion we've set aside an area in our basement for things we no longer need but others do. When the racks are full, we bag them or stack them and donate them to organizations that serve the poor. Garage sales are not an option—if it's not good enough to give it away, we throw it away or recycle it.

God, speaking through Moses, underscores His opposition to the lack of care and concern for the poor that a "garage-sale mentality" produces: "When you reap the harvest of your land, do not reap to the very edges of your field or gather the gleanings of your harvest. Do not go over your vineyard a second time or pick up the grapes that have fallen. Leave them for the poor and the foreigner. I am the LORD your God" (Lev. 19:9–10 NIV).

Support systemic changes in our cultural and political posture toward the poor. Nobel Prize-winning economist Joseph Stiglitz, author of *The Price of Inequality*, argues that it costs us more to maintain economic inequalities than it would to fix them. We treat the iconic literary character Robin Hood as a hero, but stealing from the rich to give to the poor is not an American Dream value. It violates our constitutional conviction that all are created equal, and therefore have equal agency in pursuing economic stability. This is an American belief, but not rooted in Scripture—the poor depend on the rich to rebalance the scales of opportunity. Speaking through the prophet Isaiah, God urges His people to spend their currency on the disadvantaged: "If you offer yourself to the hungry and satisfy the need of the afflicted, then your light will rise in darkness, and your gloom will become like midday" (Isa. 58:10 NASB). And Jesus reminds His disciples: "Sell your possessions and give to charity; make yourselves money belts that do not wear out, an inexhaustible treasure in heaven" (Luke 12:33 NASB).

---

2. Give dignity to the poor, in a "protest of beauty" against the meritocracy.

When we advocate for dignity among the poor—investing in their agency over the oppressive forces that are tamping down their contributions to society—we join the apostle Paul in his rebellion against the "kingdom of darkness" (Col. 1:13). Jesus, says Paul, "has purchased our freedom and [forgiven] our sins" (v. 14) so that we can offer the poor a "share in the inheritance that belongs to his people, who live in the light" (v. 12).

My wife serves in a nonprofit organization called Project Worthmore—its mission is to come alongside refugees and immigrants, the poorest of the poor, to help them learn English, find jobs, navigate American bureaucracy and the legal system, and raise their level of education. Many of the people she serves are traumatized by what they have been through, and have a long road back to a place where they can feel stable and safe. They are recovering from traumatic emotional injuries, and they need people who will walk with them until they have been strengthened enough to walk on their own. Likewise, our church has a companion ministry called CrossPurpose, a job-training program developed in partnership with the congregation and located on church property. These efforts are designed to come alongside the poor as compassionate peers—not the "savers" and the "saved." The goal is to re-dignify those whose life narrative has undermined their agency.

At the core of dignity-giving is the spiritual practice of "naming." To name someone means to *see* them—to appreciate the beauty of their created-in-God's-image reflection and intentionally highlight it. We do this when we personalize the poor—we call them by name because we know their name, and honor the sacred story that sits behind that name. This means that our response to poverty in the world is to dignify the stories of those who are suffering because of it. We slow down to pay attention to the stories of those who live on the margins—to lift our head, make eye contact, and listen. We interact with them as individuals, not numbers or "illegals," if their immigration status is undetermined. We value our presence with them over the resources we can offer, but offer those resources anyway. When Jesus invites Himself to a meal at the home of the hated tax collector Zacchaeus, He is telegraphing His interest in the man's story—his *full* story.

3. Squirm through the eye of your needle.

After Jesus re-explains what He's done in His interaction with the rich young ruler, the disciples are even more upset by His assessment of the rich. Why? *Because none of the disciples are poor.* In fact, in comparison to the average person living in their culture, they're rich. Peter, Andrew, James, and John are middle-class commercial fishermen who own their own small businesses. Judas has a long history and experience in finance. Not only is Matthew not poor, he's super rich—making a fortune as a collaborating tax collector for the Roman occupiers. Simon the Zealot grew up in a rich family. When Nathanael is called by Jesus, he's relaxing under a tree in the middle of the day, when all his peers are at work. Jesus Himself grows up in a middle-class home, the son of a skilled *tekton* (stone mason) who has plenty of work from the large rock quarry midway between Nazareth and Sepphoris.[12]

So, why does Jesus appear to banish the rich from the kingdom of God? The disciples (and us!) misunderstand the point He is trying to make with the rich young ruler. It's not his riches Jesus is after, it's the neediness those riches replace. If the young man were to sell all that he owns and give the proceeds to the poor, he would then be needy, just as the poor are. And in his neediness he would be prepared to follow Jesus— he would find his way through the eye of the needle. Though Jesus' disciples are not needy on the surface, they are all desperate underneath the surface. Peter watches Jesus miraculously fill his nets with fish, and his first reaction is, "Oh Lord, please leave me—I'm such a sinful man" (Luke 5:8). Matthew is rich, but vilified as a traitor by everyone. John communicates his fundamental gratitude for the way Jesus has rescued him when he refers to himself, repeatedly, as "the disciple Jesus loves." James and John are so driven by insecurity that they deputize their mother to leverage positions of honor with Jesus. Thomas seems to orbit outside the inner circle of disciples, uncertain of his place and full of questions. Judas is hiding a pattern of secret sin.

Our way into the kingdom of God is clear—get in touch with the poverty of our spirit by re-exploring our story. To discover the neediness that sits at our core as humans, the longing left over from our relational separation from God in the garden of Eden, we have to be more honest about the pain we experience in childhood. When we surface and embrace the wounding that marks our own story, we find our poverty. And when we do, we uncover the grace that is remaking our brokenness. Trauma therapist Adam Young says: "God honors our family narratives; they are the soil in which Truth is planted. In Philippians 3, Paul is saying that until he names the ways he has suffered because of the sin of others, he can't experience the rescue and soothing of God. We need other people to bear witness to our story and speak into it."[13]

When we pull back the veil from our story, inviting others to see it, we also expose the roots of our dependence. And when we embrace our neediness and live with an everyday awareness of it, Jesus is saying He will lead us through the eye of the needle, the gateway into His kingdom. If we have not yet done this, we still can. Of course, initially it's scary—but that fear will settle down after we start sharing the truth of our own narrative. The goal is not to revisit our pain, but to reclaim our neediness.

As a child growing up in a home with parents distracted by their own pain, with no accurate relational mirrors reflecting back the truth about who I was, I embraced a deep belief: *There's an empty void at the center of my soul, and I must make sure no one discovers this truth about me.* Of course, living inside this belief formed me into a person who fundamentally feared his own emptiness, and that deeply impacted my early marriage, leading to a painful separation and (eventually) a breakthrough leveraged by counseling. I've shared this aspect of my narrative over and over with others, embracing and re-embracing my fundamental dependence on Jesus for the solid foundation of my identity.

---

4. Alter your media consumption to immerse yourself in the world of the poor.

We're profoundly influenced by the company we keep, and that includes our media consumption. Americans are engaged with media, on average, more than seven hours every day.[14] Its forming influence in our lives is obvious. So, add the voices of the poor into your everyday media-forming mix. We're profoundly influenced by the company we keep, and that includes our media consumption. Americans are engaged with media, on average, more than seven hours every day. Its forming influence in our lives is obvious. So, add a broad spectrum voices that advocate for the poor into your everyday media-forming mix—even if some of those voices come from Christian media "neighborhoods" or secular organizations that are off the beaten path for you:

- For a global perspective on efforts to serve the poor and renovate the political and economic systems that breed poverty, read *Borgen Magazine* (borgenmagazine.com) or back issues of *Pathways Magazine*, published by the Stanford Center on Poverty & Inequality (inequality.stanford.edu).
- Watch films and documentaries that open a portal into the lives of the poor, the immigrant, and the refugee—three recent examples for us have been:

  - *The Swimmers*, following the harrowing journey of two young Syrian refugees trying to escape overwhelming violence in their country
  - *Lion*, the acclaimed film about a five-year-old Indian boy who gets lost and must fend for himself until he's adopted by an Australian couple
  - *The Pursuit*, a documentary about efforts to lift up the poor around the world, hosted by economist and Harvard Professor of Leadership Arthur Brooks

No streaming service has a sub-category for "documentaries on poverty," but you can Google that descriptor and you'll find them on YouTube, Amazon Prime, Apple TV, and other sites.

  - Read contemporary books such as Joseph Stiglitz's *The Price of Inequality*, or *The Locust Effect* by International Justice Mission founder Gary Haugen, or *Under the Affluence* by activist Tim Wise, or *The Hole in Our Gospel* by World Vision's Richard Stearns. Consider classics such as a *The Little Flowers of St. Francis* by Ugolino Brunforte and *Rich Christians in an Age of Hunger* by the grandfather of Christian activism for the poor, Ron Sider.
  - Listen to podcasts such as *The Poverty Podcast* by the World Bank (at worldbank.org), or *City Limits: A Poverty Project* (at npr.org/podcasts), or *From Poverty to Power*, hosted by Duncan Green (frompoverty.oxfam.org.uk).
  - Get on the email list for International Justice Mission (at ijm.org).

Or sign up for newsletters from World Vision (worldvision.org), Compassion (compassion.com), or the Poverty Action Lab (povertyactionlab.org) cofounded by 2019 Nobel Prize winners Abhijit Banerjee, Esther Duflo, and Michael Kremer—honored for their pioneering approach to alleviating global poverty.

Jesus told people who wanted to follow Him that "foxes have holes and birds of the air have nests, but the Son of Man has no place to lay his head" (Matt. 8:20 NASB). Jesus embraced His own neediness by making Himself dependent on His Father in every way. He didn't just identify with the poor, He *was* poor. Jesus chose to be dependent on others for housing, for His Father to provide food, and on others (primarily women) to fund His ministry. He chose a life of dependence. The God who owns everything owned nothing while He walked on earth.

Catholic missionary Dr. Tom Catena serves more than a half-million people as the only permanent doctor in the Nuba Mountains of South Sudan. The impoverished locals, under constant bombardment from government bombing campaigns, nicknamed Catena "Jesus Christ." Why? A village chief explained that "Jesus healed the sick, made the blind see, and helped the lame walk—and that is what Dr. Tom does every day."[15] When we are known as followers of Jesus, we will be known as people who have a heart for the poor.

Reflection/Discussion Questions for Individuals or Small Groups

The Marginalization of the Poor

- In general, have you seen wealth as a sign of God's favor? Why or why not?

- Jesus has a "preference for the poor"—how does that challenge your worldview, or support your worldview?

- Poverty can be crushing and destructive—so why does Jesus seem to lift it up as blessing?

- How would you characterize your relationship to poverty in your context, and in the world?

- How have you experienced poverty of any kind in your own life? How has that experience impacted your relationship with Jesus?

- When you think about the passion Jesus has for the poor, and the priority He sets for caring for the poor, what do you know about His heart? Explain.

4

The Problem with Principles

✳ ✳ ✳

"My dear Martha, you are worried and upset over all these details! There is only one thing worth being concerned about."
LUKE 10:41–42

One night, I sat with a small gathering of invited Christian leaders as theologian and USC professor of philosophy Dr. Dallas Willard targeted the fallacies behind "following biblical principles" as a path to transformation—the most common and widely accepted discipleship strategy in the church:

> Researchers reveal a dismal picture of the ordinary Christian. [They] tend to identify salvation as forgiveness of sins through means of correct doctrine—biblical principles. But is our standard for salvation based on biblical principles or intimacy with God? Go back to Jesus' teaching in Matthew 5:20. Our righteousness must surpass that of the Pharisees, or we won't enter the kingdom of heaven—now, not later. If we try to live our life by rules, we'll fail. We have a view of belief that isn't really belief—it is profession of principles. We think profession is

pleasing to God. But the reason the Pharisees are driven to hypocrisy is because they're obsessed with doing the right thing. It's all about doing.[1]

Willard is pointing out a kind of home-blindness embedded in the church's conventional strategies for encouraging Christian maturity. To understand those strategies, we can study commonalities in the most popular sermon topics among US pastors—when we do, we discover that a "biblical principles" approach to transformation dominates.[2] A principle is a "proposition that serves as the foundation for a system of belief." And a *biblical* principle is a proposition drawn from Scripture that we're to understand, embrace, and then "apply to our life." On the ministry-resourcing site Sermon Search, four of the seven most-searched sermon topics target "propositional" principles—"life change," "habits," "tithing," and "character-based."[3] And the remaining three topics—"book-of-the-Bible studies," "theology," and "seasonal"—offer easy on-ramps into principle-focused teaching.

Pastors working from this common menu of sermon topics are shaping their congregants' norms and expectations for spiritual growth. Over the course of a long sojourn in the church, I've been involved in Methodist, Evangelical Covenant, Charismatic, Presbyterian, Catholic, Southern Baptist, Anglican, Lutheran, Nazarene, and Assemblies of God churches. And while it's not a careful data analysis of sermon themes, I can sum up my five decades of church teaching on faith-growth simply: *The church wants me to believe that mastering biblical principles will lead to maturity. I can expect to be transformed when I understand biblical principles and apply them to my life.*

So, what's the problem with this understand-and-apply formula?

As Willard suggests, when we invest our hope in principles to transform our lives, we have subtly shifted the focus to our own willpower and away from an abiding dependence on Jesus. If you're a churchgoer, try this personal experiment:

1) Ask yourself what last Sunday's sermon was about—your "understanding" of it.

2) Now ask yourself what you were supposed to "apply" from that sermon.

3) Now ask yourself if you've applied any of that.

For almost all of us, this simple experiment yields discouraging results. Why? Because understand-and-apply as a formation strategy is fatally flawed. It leads us to assume that mere human understanding leads to growth, and that our growth in Christ is dependent on our ability or willingness to apply truth to our lives. On both counts we human beings have a dismal track record. Even Satan understands biblical truth, for example, but mere understanding has not transformed him. In contrast to this understand-and-apply strategy, Jesus promotes and models an entirely different path to transformation.

Author, pastor, and theologian Ray Ortlund spotlights the core teaching of Jesus on transformation: "Remain in me, and I will remain in you. For a branch cannot produce fruit if it is severed from the vine, and you cannot be fruitful unless you remain in me" (John 15:4). Then Ortlund offers this: "Why did Jesus say this? Because our default is to do Christianity without Him. So He told us plainly how it *really* works."[4]

By setting our sights on mastering biblical principles, embracing the understand-and-apply mindset for "personal transformation," we are unconsciously "trying to do Christianity without Him" by investing ourselves in try-harder-to-do-better mechanics, as Ortlund points out. When we do, we edit out Jesus' central mission in our life—the restoration of relational intimacy with the Trinity. Jesus didn't come to help us perform better in life; He came to reestablish a bride/bridegroom relationship with His beloveds. As intimacy is restored we gain access to the life of Jesus, which naturally produces a bumper-crop of fruit in our life. This is the fruit that understanding and applying our principles promises to produce, but can't apart from a source of strength that is far beyond our own.

When we "yoke" ourselves to the understand-and-apply strategy, we are trying to pull an over-filled oxcart (piled with moral and religious expectations) in our own strength—our poor "performance" is no surprise, because our willpower is not up to the task. But Jesus is not prodding us to try harder to be better—He's inviting us to abide in Him, living out of His strength as we "take on His yoke." He says: "Come to me, all of you who are weary and carry heavy burdens, and I will give you rest. Take my yoke upon you. Let me teach you, because I am humble and gentle at heart, and you will find rest for your souls. For my yoke is easy to bear, and the burden I give you is light" (Matt. 11:28–30).

In light of the strength we lack, we invite the strength He has.

Jesus is inviting an intimate partnership—to be co-yoked with Him because our "pulling power" pales in comparison to His. We are, metaphorically, a mouse yoked to an elephant. And that's the only way that cartful of moral expectations is going to move. His yoke is "easy" because He's a humble, gentle elephant who will do most of the pulling on our moral oxcart. To return to Jesus' branch-in-Vine metaphor—as we fix ourselves on abiding (or remaining) in intimacy with Jesus, we open a conduit for His life to flow into our life. When that happens, fruit grows on the ends of our branches. In light of the strength we lack, we invite the strength He has.

A focus on mastering principles, in contrast, means we try harder and harder to master our human will. It's a test of our core strength, with each new principle added to our oxcart making it harder to pull. But this willpower-based approach to achieving goodness, fueled by demanding disciplines that are impossible for us to maintain, is the very practice Jesus lambasted in the Pharisees, over and over: "[Religious leaders] crush people with unbearable religious demands and never lift a finger to ease the burden" (Matt. 23:4). The Pharisees, Jesus makes clear, have replaced worship—or beholding the beauty of God—with "religious demands." They have made religious performance, or trying harder to be better, into a god.

On most Sundays we're handed a (three-point) barbell of biblical principles, weighted with "life applications" that subtly urge us to try harder to be better—no wonder we feel the burden of "unbearable religious demands."

- *While I'm striving to be a more loving person, I remember I'm supposed to do that in a spirit of joy . . .*

- *I'm worried our home isn't as peaceful as it's supposed to be, and maybe I'm the reason why—I've got to lean into that . . .*
- *If I just had more patience and kindness toward others, then maybe they'd experience more of the good person I know I really am . . .*
- *And, of course, I'm not as faithful as I should be with my prayer and study time—I just need to be gentle with myself about that, I know I'll find the self-control I need . . . tomorrow.*

When these convictions pile up inside, it's fundamentally tempting to muscle-up the strength and willpower to (once more) scrabble up the mountain of our "religious demands." But if Jesus promises that the "yoke" He's offering us will be easy to bear, and "the burden I give you is light" (Matt. 11:30), why doesn't this feel easy and light? Our well-meaning efforts to will ourselves into "better Christians" can feel like we're dragging a pyramid. If our burdens are heavy, *maybe He didn't give them to us.* Maybe, when our sights are set on *remaining* in Jesus, it's *supposed* to feel easy. Not easy in the conventional sense—but easy in the way a healthy fruit tree naturally produces fruit. When the tree's roots are planted in good soil (deeper and deeper into the heart of Jesus), soaked with life-giving water (inviting the Spirit's guidance and encouragement), and pruned by a master gardener (yielded to the Father's discipline), fruit is the organic outcome. When our focus is on abiding, not trying harder to be better, then the apostle Paul's menu of "Spirit fruit" from Galatians 5 (you'll find them all in my rundown of "supposed-to's" that precedes this paragraph) are primarily the produce of our abiding, not the results of our superior willpower.

Those in the church who assume faith maturity is catalyzed through disciplined principles are, simply, repeating the mistakes of the Pharisees, who prioritized the willful exercise of righteousness and pointed to their own strength as a model of success. It's not that we're unaware of our areas of weakness and our need for personal growth, or that we assume change will happen without effort. But understand-and-apply overinvests faith and trust in our agency; branch-in-the-Vine abiding recognizes that our agency is never enough.

Of course, the truths practiced and embodied by Jesus have merit in our lives—the problem is when our determination to follow these principles becomes a functional replacement for following Jesus. Principle-keeping exercises a gravitational pull on us. Since the fall of Adam and Eve, we are fundamentally enticed by self-righteousness. The promise of the serpent in the garden is simple—*you can be like gods.* And the church's obsession with understanding and applying principles feeds into our deepest temptation—that it's better to trust in our own resources and strength than to trust in God's resources and strength.

Paul, himself a recovering principle-addict, says it clearly (I've added the "connecting tissue" in brackets): "The law of Moses [principle-based religious commands] was unable to save us because of the weakness of our sinful nature. . . . For the sinful nature is always hostile to God. It never did obey God's laws, and it never will [because principle-keeping can't pull the heavy oxcart of righteousness]. That's why those who are still under the control of their sinful nature can never please God [by trying harder to be better]. But you are not controlled by your sinful nature. You are controlled by the Spirit if you have the Spirit of God living in you [yoked to Him in intimate relationship, making our burden light]. . . . And Christ lives within you [naturally producing the fruit that principle-keeping promises we'll get if we try harder], so even though your body will die because of sin, the Spirit gives you life" (Rom. 8:3, 7–10).

We want to feast on the fruits of life well-lived, but we'd prefer to set the table and supply the menu on our own—the promise of principle-keeping entices us to believe this is possible.

Our Favorite Relational Alternative

When Jesus pays an unannounced visit to His friends Mary and Martha, He blunts Martha's attempts to shame her sister into helping with the dinner details. We feel a vague and kindred empathy for the uber-responsible, servant-hearted woman who's just trying to set a good table for an important guest. Mary is doing the right thing, because Jesus tells us she is. But why is Martha doing the *wrong* thing?

86

Most of us, most of the time, would agree with the principled way Martha sacrifices herself to serve. She is following the religious values of hospitality she was brought up on—to honor her guests with a generous offering of food and drink, and a well-ordered and welcoming home. Mary, meanwhile, has concerned herself only with plumbing the depths of Jesus. She is hanging on His every word, eager to drink in His heart. And Jesus, though conscious of Martha's irritation over her sister's apparently entitled attitude, says He won't take from Mary the one thing that really matters. And that one thing is *relational intimacy*. Martha wants Mary to trade what she's doing—relating to Jesus—for practicing the imperatives dictated by her culture's religious principles. Both are trying to honor Jesus, but one of them is investing in relational vulnerability *with Him* while the other is investing in activity on *behalf of Him*.

In the church, we can't bring ourselves to quit our love affair with understanding and applying principles. We are so deep into Martha-ing that we don't realize how anemic our Mary-ing is. Learning and following principles as a substitute for abiding in Jesus offers us a template for Christian living that is systemic and controllable, our favorite alternatives to real relationship with God (which requires improvisation and is unpredictable).

As Ray Ortlund points out, Jesus wants us to attach to Him like a branch grafted into a vine. This is what Mary is offering Him—immersive attention, wonder, and relational vulnerability. The fruit of this attachment is passion, an outflow of our heart/soul/mind/strength investment in the beauty of Jesus. Mary is beholding Jesus; Martha is working hard to perform for Him, and upset that her efforts are not enough. The passion we see in Mary is a conduit for the kind of spiritual fruits that look like disciplines but are actually the natural produce of relational intimacy with Jesus. "Those who remain in me, and I in them," says Jesus, "will produce much fruit. For apart from me you can do nothing" (John 15:5). And by "nothing," He means "zero." Later, Paul explains: "Therefore, my brothers and sisters, you also were put to death in regard to the Law through the body of Christ, so that you might belong to another, to Him who was raised from the dead, in order that we might bear fruit for God" (Rom. 7:4 NASB).

Botanists tell us that the bond between the grafted branch and the vine transforms the branch into a miniature version of the parent tree.[5] This is why Jesus can make this ludicrous statement with a straight face: "Truly, truly, I say to you, the one who believes in Me, the works that I do, he will do also; and greater works than these he will do; because I am going to the Father" (John 14:12 NASB). If our attachment to Him essentially makes us a miniature version of the parent tree, the fruit we produce will be like His own, and even greater. Grafted fruit trees produce bigger, tastier fruit—and they produce it more quickly.[6] Of course, our grafted spiritual bond requires time to "take," just as it does in the organic world. But the result is the graft, over time, becomes one with the vine.

So Mary is not *disciplining* herself to sit and enjoy her beloved Jesus; she can't help herself. Her heart is captured by His heart. Jesus will not tolerate what Martha is pressuring Mary to do, just as He won't tolerate our substitution of intimacy with Him for principle-keeping.

Only relational intimacy produces the depth-of-soil needed for the seeds of faith to grow sustaining roots.

In His parable of the farmer scattering seed, Jesus tells the story of a sower who indiscriminately spreads his seed over a field, covering four types of soil—only one of which is truly fertile. The second soil is likely a veiled reference to the failed "growth environment" created by the Pharisees, who use religious principles to coerce their followers into righteous living. "Other seeds fell on shallow soil with underlying rock [the religious laws and principles pushed by the Pharisees]. The seeds sprouted quickly because the soil was shallow [people obey out of fear and guilt and shame]. But the plants soon wilted under the hot sun, and since they didn't have deep roots, they died [fear, guilt, and shame don't produce deep growth]" (Matt. 13:5–6). Only relational intimacy produces the depth-of-soil needed for the seeds of faith to grow sustaining roots. A faith planted in principles is like planting in shallow soil—what little growth we see quickly wilts.

Oxford economics professor John Kay says: "The process in which well-defined and prioritized objectives are broken down into specific states and actions whose progress can be monitored and measured is not the reality of how people find fulfillment in their lives, create great art, establish great societies or build good businesses."[7] In other words, following principles and measuring our progress never produces the deep-impact results that following our passion produces—this is what Jesus is trying to help Martha understand.

The Handbook Reduction

In the church, we often refer to the Bible as a "handbook for life"—while it offers plenty of guidance for our everyday challenges, this reduces the purpose of Scripture to a principle to-do list. Theologian and Boston College professor Dr. Peter Kreeft compares reading the Bible to standing under "a big sprig of [God's] mistletoe."[8] It's a love story, set against the epic backdrop of betrayal, brokenness, and costly redemption. So, when we treat the message of the Bible as a searchable index of solutions for life's problems, with corresponding principles that must be practiced to guarantee success, we obliterate its central romance. The difference between a handbook and a love story is the difference between a tutoring session and a date night. One produces a grade, the other produces a passion.

David Zahl, pastor and director of Mockingbird Ministries, says: "If the ultimate message [of the Bible] comes across that you need to be different, and that Christianity is a means to a different end, like a personal transformation, then you're just in competition with all sorts of other spiritual 'products' . . . I grew up with a picture of Christianity that was very much a hospital, or a hospice. . . . Maybe it's something American or maybe it's something just human, but we want to make it into a boot camp for new glory. . . . At the center of our faith . . . is a God who gave up agency, who gave up status, who was crucified, who was executed, who was only influential by lack of His influence."[9]

We can track our addiction to principles, and our reductionist reading of the Bible, back to the transaction Adam and Eve made in the garden of Eden. Let's revisit the particulars.

Remember, the serpent tells the man and woman they won't die if they eat the forbidden fruit—instead, "God knows that your eyes will be opened as soon as you eat it, and you will be like God, knowing both good and evil" (Gen. 3:5). The issue is control—who should be in control of "the knowledge of good and evil"? Until this moment, Adam and Eve live in trusting abandon to the God-standard for goodness, but the serpent preys on the perceived unfairness of this arrangement: *What is keeping you from deciding good and bad for yourself? Your jealous and controlling God wants no competition from you—that's why He's forcing His standards on you.* At the heart of this temptation is the central issue of our lives—in whom will we trust?

The "first couple" seizes the control that the serpent's petty, stingy, and suspicious god has kept from them—now they can follow their own principles of goodness, trusting themselves to construct a moral ecosystem outside of their dependence on God. The Trinity quickly diagnoses the evil that will result from this self-determination: "Look, the human beings have become like us, knowing both good and evil. What if they reach out, take fruit from the tree of life, and eat it? Then they will live forever!" (Gen. 3:22). Like a self-driving car plagued by software bugs, it won't be long before Adam and Eve run humanity off a cliff. They must have an endpoint to their life or they will become like the serpent, an embodied evil. Death is introduced as a vital boundary around a humanity that will now and forever create its own systems of right and wrong.

Following the principles we source from our own "knowledge of good and evil" means our relational conduit for goodness—our intimate attachment to God—is cut off. And without it, just three chapters later in Genesis, the whole world is engulfed in a sin-cleansing flood. "The LORD observed the extent of human wickedness on the earth, and he saw that everything they thought or imagined was consistently and totally evil." And then this heartbreaking confession: "So the LORD was sorry he had ever made them and put them on the earth" (Gen. 6:5–6). Though God relents from total annihilation when Noah "finds favor" with Him, the rest of the created world is wiped clean by the reset button.

Now, though we are limited by death in our ability to impose our own forms of goodness (the mid-century secular communist utopia that quickly devolved into autocracy and wide-scale purges, for example), we still have a problem. Only God is good, but we insist we can source and manage our own goodness apart from Him. Because we have eaten from the tree of the knowledge of good and evil, we believe our goodness is inherent—we can substitute our own principle-keeping for dependence on God.

In the West, social science researchers call this system of principle-keeping "moralistic therapeutic deism," or MTD.[10] It's a description coined by academics who launched a massive, groundbreaking project called the National Study of Youth and Religion. It means that, for a huge swath of American Christians:

- God is intentionally distant in our lives, not interested in a relationship
- People are supposed to be good and moral toward one another by exercising their own strength and willpower
- The purpose of life is to exercise your own agency to find happiness and feel good about yourself
- There are no universal and absolute moral truths
- Only "good people" go to heaven, and most people are good enough
- God places very limited demands on people—we're to live out our "good person" mandate on our own

Three out of four self-identifying Christians in the US embrace MTD as their spiritual worldview—a template for living out their "knowledge of good and evil" (though, of course they don't use the phrase itself). Those who live through the lens of MTD don't believe people are foundationally sinful and therefore don't believe redemption through Jesus is all that necessary (91 percent). And three-quarters believe their good behavior will determine their entry into heaven.[11]

Researcher George Barna observes: "The fact that a greater percentage of people who call themselves Christian draw from Moralistic Therapeutic Deism than draw from the Bible says a lot about the state of the Christian Church in America, in all of its manifestations. . . . Simply and objectively stated, Christianity in this nation is rotting from the inside out. . . . It seems that most of these folks want to do the right thing; they simply have been led down the wrong paths toward achieving that end."[12]

Barna's use of "Christianity" here implies that a religious system is out of whack. But the deeper truth is that we have edited Jesus to fit our post-Eden beliefs about our autonomy from God. MTD describes a willful myth—a life defined by the pursuit of goodness but fundamentally disconnected from its only source. It is disembodied goodness.

"A good tree can't produce bad fruit," explains Jesus, "and a bad tree can't produce good fruit. A tree is identified by its fruit. . . . A good person produces good things from the treasury of a good heart, and an evil person produces evil things from the treasury of an evil heart" (Luke 6:43–45). Goodness, then, is sourced from a flowing river of good in our heart. And the Trinity is its only headwaters. This means that our common belief in our own goodness, relationally separate from the Spirit of God's replenishing reserves, is ridiculous in the extreme. Jesus is offering us a heart transplant, not a pep talk. But the vast majority of us believe a pep talk is all we really need, because our own goodness (propelled and ensured by our determination to master biblical principles) is so substantial that a little boost every now and then is sufficient.

This is likely why self-help books are the fastest-growing literary genre in the world, a $10.5 billion-dollar industry.[13] Here's an interesting comparison—over the last decade, church attendance has declined by 10 percent[14] while sales of self-help books have grown by 11 percent.[15] If the church has devolved into a place to "profess principles"—replacing discipleship (a growing intimacy with Jesus) with trying harder to be better—then maybe those who are leaving the church have simply decided they can find all that in a well-crafted self-help book instead. If the pastor's job is to urge us toward self-improvement, using biblical principles as goads, why not simply read a good Brené Brown book (or listen to her podcast) instead?

The self-help disciplines embedded in the way we're typically urged to practice biblical principles subtly invite us to reclaim our identity formation from God—to read or think or will our way to meaning and significance. Resisting this lure to self-determination, Isaiah cries out to God in humble submission: "We are the clay, and you are the potter. We all are formed by your hand" (Isa. 64:8). Isaiah is yielding himself to the force of God's love flowing through his vulnerable and dependent attachment. When we trust our principles to form us, not the hand of God, the clay takes over from the potter.

The Deification of Data

Closely related to our elevation of principles is our belief that knowledge (the more the better) is our salvation. Toward the end of his pandemic-era novel *The Lake Wobegon Virus*, author, humorist, and *Prairie Home Companion* host Garrison Keillor has his alter ego in the story offer a spontaneous Independence Day speech at his fictional hometown's annual picnic. He's reveling in the ecstasy of freshly prepared sweet corn on the cob, but he's also gutting our expectation that gaining knowledge and practicing principles—the "data" of our faith—will save us.

> There are four main pleasures in life—the pleasure of knowledge, the pleasure of walking with God, and the pleasure that some of you thought of first. . . . And then there is sweet corn, fresh from the field, quickly husked, briefly boiled, buttered and salted. And here we are, drunk on it. Out of our minds with happiness. . . . It's my belief that no person can have all four pleasures. And if I had to choose which to sacrifice, I would give up knowledge. Because, as anyone can tell you, it only leads to misery. Because, with increased knowledge comes the knowledge that many people know much more than you. And they are [idiots]. Absolute nincompoops. And they have no idea of their nincompoopery.[16]

When we join the knowledge rat race, we expect to be rewarded with emotional, intellectual, social, financial, and spiritual benefits. But, as Keillor observes, we've been over-sold. If "right knowledge" alone is transformational, Jesus certainly would've had a better track record with His closest followers, who repeatedly misunderstand His mission, priorities, and values.

In a letter to the Roman emperor Antoninus Pius, the early church theologian Justin Martyr explains the relational (not data-driven) propellant behind the rapid spread of Christianity: "We formerly rejoiced in uncleanness of life, but now love only chastity; before we used the magic arts, but now dedicate ourselves to the true and unbegotten God; before we loved money and possessions more than anything, but now we share what we have and to everyone who is in need; before we hated one another and killed one another and would not eat with those of another race, but now since the manifestation of Christ, we have come to a common life and pray for our enemies and try to win over those who hate us without just cause."[17]

Knowledge is a *fruit* of a relational reality, not its foundation. This is true theologically, practically, and organically. In a long-term study of the factors that influence adolescents to embrace a lifelong, "devoted" faith in God, a research team led by Notre Dame sociologist of religion Dr. Christian Smith discovered these five imperatives:

1. Frequent personal prayer
2. Strong parental religion—more religiously committed parents
3. High importance of religious faith in everyday life
4. Few religious doubts
5. Has a history of "powerful religious experiences"[18]

Aside from #4, which implies that greater knowledge may be an effective way to counter what we might call "apologetic challenges," the other factors are all relational. The study's authors sum up: "In order to sustain high levels of religious commitment and practice during the emerging adult years, several distinct factors seem especially important: first, strong *relational modeling and support* for religious commitment; second, genuine *internalization* of religious significance; and third, the *personal practice* of religious faith."[19] To behold Jesus means that our relational intimacy with Him is fed by our knowledge and experience of Him. Knowledge is a means to a relational end, not fuel for my try-harder-to-be-better aspirations. Put another way—*knowing about* is not the same as *knowing*.

In contrast to these findings, and to Jesus' own vigorous focus on the heart over the head, the contemporary church has elevated what amounts to a knowledge dump as its primary strategy for faith maturity. Sermons are often delivery vehicles for principles, and most forms of youth and adult ministry are dominated by the attempted transfer of knowledge from a more knowledgeable person to a less knowledgeable person. Spiritual maturity, the outcome of a relational infection, is repurposed into a knowledge quest that can comfortably exist outside of any intimacy with God at all. It's in the context of a trusting relationship with Jesus, following His guidance in our real-world decisions, and acting on what we know to be true about His heart, that we are more and more transformed into His image. He wants our heart, because the head alone will never catalyze our renovation. And we give our hearts to Him when we behold His beauty. That's why a church intent on creating a transformational ecosystem would do well to focus *all it does* on beholding the beauty of Jesus.

George MacDonald, the Scottish pastor and mystic—the man C. S. Lewis called "my master"—said this about the mission of Jesus in our life: "It was not for our understanding, but our will, that Christ came. He who does that which he sees, shall understand; he who is set upon understanding rather than doing, shall go on stumbling and mistaking and speaking foolishness."[20] James the apostle says it this way: "Don't just listen to God's word. You must do what it says. Otherwise, you are only fooling yourselves. For if you listen to the word and don't obey, it is like glancing at your face in a mirror. You see yourself, walk away, and forget what you look like" (James 1:22–24).

The Gamble We Don't Know We're Making

In contemporary culture, we have obviously progressed in our knowledge of things—technologically and scientifically. But try-harder strategies tied to principle-driven transformation have not progressed us as moral people (despite what we'd like to believe about ourselves). We have gambled on the human will as the engine of change, and lost.

In his 1964 acceptance speech for the Nobel Peace Prize, Martin Luther King Jr. observed: "Modern man has brought this whole world to an awe-inspiring threshold of the future. He has reached new and astonishing peaks of scientific success . . . a dazzling picture of modern man's scientific and technological progress. Yet, in spite of these spectacular strides in science and technology, and still unlimited ones to come, something basic is missing. . . . The richer we have become materially, the poorer we have become morally and spiritually. We have learned to fly the air like birds and swim the sea like fish, but we have not learned the simple art of living together as brothers."[21]

Cultural philosopher Mark Sayers, pastor of Melbourne's Red Church, calls our addiction to principle-driven strategies in the church "Taylorism." He's referencing the Quaker management theorist and engineer Frederick Taylor, whose convictions about linear, efficient leadership structures and practices have infiltrated every facet of society, including the church. "Taylorism transformed leaders into managers who delegated tasks and supervised workers underneath them," says Sayers, "managing them to achieve the broken-up tasks in a linear fashion until the tasks are completed . . . Taylor's techniques were also applied to the realm of personal improvement. Individuals were encouraged to 'manage' their lives by aiming for personal development goals and creating 'life projects,' which were broken into achievable parts or habits to ensure productivity."[22]

Taylorism infected the church's ministry vision with a belief that "change would happen gradually, logically, and sequentially," and that "the more information and data we have, the more understanding we will have and the more empowered we will be."[23] Our transformation, then, is dependent on how well we follow the sequential imperatives that emerge from our understanding of biblical principles. This moral-code/principle path to maintaining goodness is doomed to failure because it's a bad bet. It wagers our morality against our bankrupt ability to master good and evil on our own terms.

When an exasperated Thomas tells Jesus that he and the other disciples don't know how to follow where He's going, Jesus responds: "I am the way, the truth, and the life" (John 14:5–6). Thomas is looking for the "logical, sequential" path to a renovated life. But goodness is *contained* in the person of Jesus, and possible only *through* Him. We have so edited Jesus that His approval of the self-sourced, self-righteous path to living out the moral imperatives of the kingdom of God seems self-evident. The Jesus we hear described at church is often metaphorically wagging His finger at us, urging us to try harder to be better. And when we are not better, we hide from Him or ignore Him or recast His expectations.

The weakness of our moral codes exposes the fragility of our goodness apart from intimate attachment to God. This is why Jesus sets out to intentionally undermine this Martha-over-Mary momentum in us.

A hungry crowd gathers on a hillside, peppering Jesus with questions about what they should be doing to "perform God's works" (John 6). They want food, an entertaining show, and tips and techniques for living righteously. They want to know what Jesus can do for them (sound familiar?). And Jesus' upending, even disturbing, response to their performance demands is to insist that they "eat Him," the "Bread of Life." They want principles for living out the goodness expected of them, but Jesus gives them this instead: "Whoever comes to me will never be hungry again. Whoever believes in me will never be thirsty." Jesus wants relational dependence, not principle-dependence. Goodness will flow out of us organically when we "eat" the source of all goodness.

When we consume food, we take something from outside our body, inside our body. We chew, swallow, and eventually become one with our food, as the food becomes one with us. Jesus chooses the metaphor of eating and drinking to invite us into the kind of intimacy that naturally produces goodness in us—we are what we eat. To His disciples He promises: "No, I will not abandon you as orphans—I will come to you. . . . When I am raised to life again, you will know that I am in my Father, and you are in me, and I am in you" (John 14:18–20).

A conspiratorial pack of religious leaders entraps a wayward woman, catching her in the act of adultery (John 8). The moral code of Moses' law dictates that the woman be stoned to death, so they ask Jesus: "What do you say?" Here Jesus needs a little extra time to defuse their moral IED—so He writes in the dust, and then He stands. "All right, but let the one who has never sinned throw the first stone!" And, of course, everyone slinks away, leaving the woman alone with Jesus. They have tried to dehumanize her by reducing her worth down to the moral principles she breaks or upholds. They have tied their beliefs about human dignity to her capacity to maintain foundational morality.

David French asks an important question: "If we all know that Christians aren't perfect, why does Christian sin and hypocrisy drive so many people from the faith?" He points to the Lifeway Research finding that nine out of ten evangelical Christians say they staunchly oppose abortion and sex outside of marriage, but close to half (43 percent) say Jesus was a good teacher, but not divine.[24] French concludes: "This all leads me to the complex relationship between theology, morality, and hypocrisy—and to how hypocrisy is particularly damaging when Christians are clearer about their moral stands than they are about even the identity of Jesus. When religion is primarily experienced as a moral code, moral failure undermines the faith itself."[25]

This is the misguided system of belief Jesus is exposing when He gives the conspiratorial mob the go-ahead to execute the woman caught in adultery, but requires complete moral mastery as a prerequisite. Where principles try to even the playing field, grace makes no attempt to be fair. Grace is a relational act; principle-keeping is an exercise of the will.

The Pharisees challenge Jesus, over and over, to uphold the principles embedded in "the law and the prophets." Instead, He essentially responds, *I am the law and the prophets.* Jesus describes and spotlights the truth, but more than that, He embodies it (John 14:6). He makes this distinction often, even early in His ministry: "Don't misunderstand why I have come. I did not come to abolish the law of Moses or the writings of the prophets. No, I came to accomplish their purpose" (Matt. 5:17). He is launching a new way of living, moving the people of God from an outside-in "discipline" of the truth to an inside-out "embodying" of the truth, through our intimate branch-in-the-Vine relationship with Him.

The principles that ruled Jewish life resulted in an elaborate system of self-cleansing—a way to control and prop up their goodness through human will. Follow the system, and you ensure your place in it. And we have edited Jesus' teachings into our own system of self-cleansing. After their last Passover meal together, Jesus gets up from the table, wraps Himself in a towel, and carries a basin of water to each person, washing His disciples' feet. He is inviting them out of principles (servants humble themselves before their masters, masters don't humble themselves before their servants) and into dependent relationship. Dependent relationships require vulnerability, vulnerability builds trust, and trust is the engine of faith. And "without faith it is impossible to please Him" (Heb. 11:6 NASB). That's because God is pleased when He experiences intimacy in relationship. A mutual, propelling love relationship is always the goal.

Walking the Way of (the Unedited) Jesus

What will it look like if we walk in the way of the unedited Jesus, shifting our focus away from principle-maintenance to increasing our capacity to be intimately present to Him? A menu of possible experiments, not a to-do list:

---

1. When principles are *not* a problem.

To reiterate, it's not that the truths practiced and embodied by Jesus have no traction or merit in our lives—the problem is our determination to follow these principles as a functional replacement for following Jesus. He is after relational intimacy with us, and our pursuit of linear paths to incremental improvement thwarts that. When a principle leads directly into greater intimacy with Jesus, it is serving its proper function. When it leads directly to greater self-reliance and detachment from Jesus, we have used it for evil. An evil is anything we do that is "opposed to God, that which is the opposite of God, and that which is contrary to God."[26]

Jesus makes this point when He spotlights what is and isn't good about the way the Pharisees live their lives: "The teachers of religious law and the Pharisees are the official interpreters of the law of Moses. So practice and obey whatever they tell you, but don't follow their example. For they don't practice what they teach" (Matt. 23:2–3). The law of Moses, properly lived, leads to a deeper intimacy with God. Instead, the Pharisees have turned the law into a Points System for ranking goodness and status. Once we put ourselves in charge of building a scaffolding for goodness in our life, we promote ourselves as gods. And now we are on the doorstep of evil. This is exactly why Jesus emphasizes, "Only God is good."

Here's how honoring principles, but not following them, works: Integrity is a long-honored biblical principle. We all want to live in integrity, in all circumstances and no matter what it costs us. And yet we don't. And when we are honest about that, we have two choices: 1) promise to redouble our efforts and try harder to master this principle—the growth strategy of the Pharisees, or 2) confess our bankrupt integrity and invite the integrity of Jesus to flow through us as we yield ourselves to Him: "I do believe [I have integrity], but help me overcome my unbelief [my lack of integrity]!" (Mark 9:24). This is the way of Jesus.

John Eldredge sums it up well: "Activity for God is not the same thing as intimacy with God. The number-one enemy of intimacy *with* God is activity *for* him."[27] This is the Mary/Martha difference re-explained.

---

2. Live in musical harmony, balancing the heart's attraction to beauty with the head's attraction to propositions.

Dr. Carl Ellis, professor of theology and culture at Reformed Theological Seminary, and a lover of improvisational jazz, offers an incisive metaphor for living in the tension between our head and our heart: "Music is very mathematical. What makes a harmony sound good? Well, that's mathematics. But I don't only *think* of music. When I hear a harmony, I don't think of it as math. I think of it as beauty. I *feel* it. We need to learn how to feel it more. Analysis is good, but sometimes things are just meant to be just enjoyed for their beauty. At the same time you've got to do more than feel. You also have to be able to analyze. But relax and let it impact you."[28]

Ellis is describing the way harmony in music impacts us, but he's also describing what harmony looks like in our relationship with Jesus. We appreciate, study, and analyze His teachings for truths that will impact our understanding of goodness (the "math" of our relationship)—but if we leave it there, we aren't following Jesus. Harmony in our relationship invites us to "taste and see" the heart of Jesus above all else, giving ourselves over to the influence and intimacy of the Spirit (the "feel" of our relationship). In His last extended mentoring session with His disciples, Jesus targets this aspect of harmony: "I will send you the Advocate—the Spirit of truth. He will come to you from the Father and will testify all about me. . . . In fact, it is best for you that I go away, because if I don't, the Advocate won't come. If I do go away, then I will send him to you. . . . When the Spirit of truth comes, he will guide you into all truth" (John 15:26; 16:7; 16:13).

To live in Spirit-dependence means we toggle our attention from the head's understanding of biblical truth to a heart experience—a "feel" for the presence of Jesus, made possible by the Advocate inside us. Eldredge, again, explains: "The mind is a beautiful instrument, but the mind was given to us to protect the heart, not to replace it. In most discipleship models, the heart is not central, but if you look at the discipleship model of Jesus the heart is very central. 'These people honor me with their lips but their hearts are far from me'—*don't give me lip service, I want your heart.* Jesus urged us to 'love the Lord your God with all your heart, soul, mind, and strength.' The mind and the heart were never meant to be in opposition to each other— they work beautifully together. Let's not make them enemies."[29]

We depend on our heart to access an in-the-moment relationship with the Spirit of Jesus. The Rabbi Inside "guides us into all truth," and then we act on that truth with an obedience driven by affection and love. For example, I know my wife hates to drink cold water, even in the summer, so I "obey" that understanding by serving her warm water, because I know something that helps me love her more sensitively. After a while, I know so many things about her heart that my "obedience" to the "truths" that matter to her develops into something like breathing. And if I forget and serve her cold water, I'm not just forgetting a preference, I'm forgetting *her.* I'm "formed" to serve what pleases her heart.

---

3. Pursue an honest reckoning about how our principle-idols are disappointing us, and lay them down.

David Foster Wallace says: "Pretty much anything else [other than God] you worship will eat you alive. If you worship money and things, if they are where you tap real meaning in life, then you will never have enough. . . . It's the truth. Worship your body and beauty and sexual allure and you will always feel ugly. . . . Worship power, you will end up feeling weak and afraid, and you will need ever more power over others to numb you to your own fear. Worship your intellect, being seen as smart, you will end up feeling stupid, a fraud, always on the verge of being found out."[30]

Whatever we worship in life gives us our sense of significance and identity. If we are disappointed, even despairing, over our inability to grow or mature, then maybe "applying principles" is "eating us alive." This is what the reinvented Pharisee Paul is getting at when he describes his own transformation to his friends in Philippi:

> All the things I once thought were so important are gone from my life. Compared to the high privilege of knowing Christ Jesus as my Master, firsthand, everything I once thought I had going for me is insignificant—dog dung. I've dumped it all in the trash so that I could embrace Christ and be embraced by him. I didn't want some petty, inferior brand of righteousness that comes from keeping a list of rules when I could get the robust kind that comes from trusting Christ—*God's* righteousness. (Phil. 3:8 MSG)

When we lay down our dependence on self-determining strength and self-help (as Paul says he did), we pick up a life of grace. We live dependent on Jesus' "unmerited favor." Later, when Paul begs Jesus to take away the "thorn in his side"—something that is keeping him from living in strength—Jesus opts for weakness instead: "My grace is all you need. My power works best in weakness" (2 Cor. 12:9). Like Paul, we decide that our best opportunity to experience strength in our life is to admit we don't have what we need, preferring instead the power that flows through us when we admit our weakness and turn to Jesus to supply what we lack.

This humble, dependent posture toward self-determination stands in stark contrast to the success narrative that has edited Jesus into a guy who gives great TED Talks, not someone who's pursuing an "I in you, you in Me" relationship. When we look to our own strength, rather than the strength that flows through us as branches abiding in the Vine, our path into wholeness is hopelessly blocked. This is exactly why Paul offers this pointed confession to his friends in Corinth:

> When I first came to you, dear brothers and sisters, I didn't use lofty

words and impressive wisdom to tell you God's secret plan. For I decided that while I was with you I would forget everything except Jesus Christ, the one who was crucified. I came to you in weakness—timid and trembling. And my message and my preaching were very plain. Rather than using clever and persuasive speeches, I relied only on the power of the Holy Spirit. I did this so you would trust not in human wisdom but in the power of God. (1 Cor. 2:1–5)

Paul knows, in his depths, that the lever of biblical principles won't transform our soul—only the life and power of the unedited Jesus can remake us from the inside out.

Reflection/Discussion Questions for Individuals or Small Groups

The Problem
with Principles

- What role have "biblical principles"—for good or bad—played in your own maturing relationship with Jesus? Explain.

- Jesus says His "yoke is easy" and His "burden is light"—is that how you would characterize your own experience of following Him, or "living the Christian life"? Why or why not?

- How have you experienced the dangers of emphasizing biblical principles as a path to maturity? How have you experienced the benefits?

- In general, what has fueled the most growth in your relationship with Jesus, and why? What are some factors or circumstances that have blocked that growth? Explain.

- One outcome of the fall of Adam and Eve is our certainty that we can decide for ourselves what's right and wrong—how have you experienced the destructive impact of that belief?

- In what ways have you unwittingly embraced the tenets of moralistic therapeutic deism in your life? How has your relationship with Jesus challenged that way of thinking?

- In your experience, what are the pros and cons of a self-help mentality?

- In our path toward maturity, Jesus elevates a growing trust in His heart over the disciplined practice of principles—how is that truth freeing for you, and how is it challenging for you?

- Why do we generally prefer head-based ways of living out our relationship with God rather than heart-based ways?

The Golden-Calfing of Materialism

* * *

**"During your lifetime you had everything
you wanted, and Lazarus had nothing."**

LUKE 16:25

In 1960, the celebrated author John Steinbeck wrote a letter to American presidential candidate Adlai Stevenson, which was later reprinted in the *Washington Post*. In it, Steinbeck says, "If I wanted to destroy a nation, I would give it too much, and I would have it on its knees, miserable, greedy, sick."[1] Because the Western church has so adopted the wider culture's obsession with materialism, tacitly ignoring Jesus' own relationship to rampant consumption, Steinbeck could have substituted "church" for "nation" and been just as prescient.

The ancient Israelites, impatient for something tangible to worship as Moses lingers on Mount Sinai for forty days, pressure Aaron into fashioning a golden calf from their melted-down jewelry. In the absence of God's identifiable movement and rescue in their life, they opt for something more material—something better able to deliver the relief and happiness they crave. Channeling this same impatience, "golden-calfism" is threaded into the fabric of our contemporary Christian identity. Though Jesus models a life of dependent simplicity—"Give us each day the food we need" (Luke 11:3)—our impatience with the promise of the Immaterial has driven us into the arms of the Material.

Our "golden calf" is the Western Christian wealth narrative.

First, some context. Late in 2020, church membership in the US dipped below the median (47 percent) for the first time, confirming the dire predictions of secularists and atheists over the last 150 years. The slide is steep, down from 50 percent in 2018 and 70 percent in 1999.[2] In the world of demography, a drop in excess of twenty points in a span of just two decades is not just an alarm bell, it's a sea change.

This downward spiral in church membership over the last two decades—like a sink-plug yanked from a drain—has an interesting overlap with the timeline of materialism's more obvious influence on our Christian worldview. One-fifth of committed Christians now believe that "meaning and purpose comes from working hard to earn as much as possible so you can make the most of life."[3] Digging deeper into the research, younger demographics (Gen Z and Millennials, who have come of age in the last two decades) are much more likely to see materialistic ideals as compatible with their Christian identity—of those under forty-five in the study, four out of ten say they're pursuing materialistic ambitions. And the overwhelming majority of those age eighteen to forty-nine (more than 80 percent) believe that God wants to prosper them financially.[4] These same generational cohorts are way overrepresented in the two-decade downturn in church membership, significantly bending the curve. As more and more young people embrace materialism as a life philosophy, they're also less likely to consider the influence of the church important.

These shifts mirror the story of the ancient Israelites. When they move away from God and toward golden-calf worship, they give in to a tactical deceit: *I have practical needs and desires in my life, and the God I can't see or hear or touch is frankly undependable. I need a concrete symbol of wealth as a tangible source of hope—I need something that will predictably deliver the safety, security, and happiness I crave.* When the people of God, then and now, embrace materialistic ideals, they abandon God as He is, crafting a god of their own making with symbols of wealth. In the same way, material ambitions are redirecting Western people—especially those who've come of age in the last two decades—away from the Jesus revealed in Scripture and toward a god who can more effectively deliver material prosperity.

Four Drivers in Our Golden-Calf Obsessions

To "follow Jesus" means we adopt His lifestyle, belief system, and core values, but we've morphed our default assumptions about consumption and material success into something diametrically opposed to His example. In one way, this is nothing new. Western culture has, for almost a century, been preoccupied with the promise of what author James Truslow first called the "American Dream"—a kind of secular religion. In his Depression-era book *Epic of America*, Truslow took a first stab at describing this constitutional entitlement (our "inalienable right" to pursue happiness): That dream "of a land in which life should be better and richer and fuller for [everyone], with opportunity for each according to [their] ability or achievement." *Parade* magazine's "genius" columnist Marilyn Vos Savant adds her own descriptors: "[It's] a house in the suburbs with a backyard for kids to play in, a patio for barbeques, a shady street, bright and obedient children, camping trips, go fishing, family cars, seeing the kids taking part in school, and church plays."

The American Dream presupposes that, in a just and democratic society, the only thing separating the haves from the have-nots is effort.[5] Author and academic Samir S. Gupte says: "Today, the American Dream is used by politicians, advertisers, athletes, and artists as a manifesto for their own purposes. Perhaps a thousand years from now, historians will examine the unique nature of the American Dream in developing America's prominence in the world and conclude that it was an epic component of human history on par with the invention of tools, or the teachings of Jesus Christ, or the ancient Greek philosophers."[6]

When Gupte compares the impact of America's "better, richer, and fuller" secular gospel to the teachings of Jesus it may seem hyperbolic, but consider.... Though almost all Americans believe their culture is too materialistic (89 percent), the overwhelming majority also say that more money is the key to the "good life" (78 percent), freedom (71 percent), and "good feelings about myself" (76 percent).[7] These are *forming* beliefs, profoundly impacting our personal and corporate identities. The New Republic's Chris Lehmann says the church has adopted its own version of American Dream-ism, practicing a brand of consumption-worship he calls the "money cult," or "the frank celebration of wealth as a spiritual virtue in American Protestantism."[8]

Among the shifts in Western culture over the last two decades that have further fueled our material ambitions as Christian-compatible, these four are significant: 1) the rise of social media, 2) the recasting of higher education as a primary conduit for future wealth, 3) the melding of discipleship with the Western success narrative, and 4) the underlying influence of Epicurean philosophy in Western culture.

---

1. The Rise of Social Media—The first online social media platforms (Myspace, Friendster, and Facebook) launched around 2003. Writing in *The Atlantic*, NYU social psychologist Dr. Jonathan Haidt observes:

> In their early incarnations, platforms such as Myspace and Facebook were relatively harmless. They allowed users to create pages on which to post photos, family updates, and links to the mostly static pages of their friends and favorite bands. In this way, early social media can be seen as just another step in the long progression of technological improvements—from the Postal Service through the telephone to email and texting—that helped people achieve the eternal goal of maintaining their social ties. But gradually, social-media users became more comfortable sharing intimate details of their lives with strangers and corporations.... They became more adept at putting on performances and managing their personal brand—activities that might impress others but that do not deepen friendships in the way that a private phone conversation will. Once social-media platforms had trained users to

spend more time performing and less time connecting, the stage was set for the major transformation, which began in 2009: the intensification of viral dynamics.[9]

When Facebook gave users the ability to "like" a post, says Haidt, the performance-driven shifts in communication already set in motion by social media became weaponized. "Keeping up with the Joneses" morphed into "Keeping up with the world." Status, wealth, and a certain veneer of happiness were now quickly and viscerally comparable, and the pressure to "have and to hold" swelled into a wave washing through all of culture, including the church.

The "viral dynamics" that have evangelized an obsession with the material have infected normal Christian practice and theology, inviting Steinbeck's "too-much-ness" to have a seat at the church's table. Princeton's Robert Wuthnow, summing up a three-year study of how Americans view money, concludes: "Although there is much lip service to decrying the overemphasis on money and materialism, in practice mammon is winning out over God."[10]

The comparison engine that social media kicked off didn't generate the norming of materialism in the church, especially among younger generations, but it has acted as an exponential magnifier. Social scientists call the psycho-social dynamic that drives our need to "keep up" materially with others "personal relative deprivation" (PRD)—it's the resentment that builds when we believe we've been "deprived of deserved outcomes compared to others."[11] An in-depth study published in Basic and Applied Social Psychology found that PRD "uniquely contributes to materialism."[12] It's an invisible virus infecting our identity at a foundational level. And social media, as Jonathan Haidt points out, has a nuclear capacity to generate PRD with greater impact than any other social dynamic in history.

2. Higher Education as a Conduit for Wealth—At my college alma mater, the messaging from the school's marketing department reflects a two-decade shift in how higher education is promoted to students—from language that conveyed an ennobling rite of passage marked by good impact in society, to a sales pitch for the passcode we need to access our ATM entitlements. The school posts and promotes something called "The [State U] Effect" with this pitch: "You came to [State U] to earn a degree and start forging your future. . . . And you want to know how [State U] graduates are faring." What follows is not a collection of graduate stories that mark their progressive good impact in business, medicine, science, education, or the arts. Instead, the school's website lists how much more in-state alumni are earning as a direct result of their degree ($2.2 billion), the percentage of students who got a job offer within six months of graduating (89 percent), the average starting salary for graduates ($49,300), and the collective household income of in-state alumni ($5.4 billion).

These metrics seem both normal and necessary in today's competitive educational environment. But what is *not promoted* is important to highlight. Note that my school is not detailing the metrics of character development, service, the pursuit of truth and knowledge, and an individual's call to invest in the bettering of society. The subtle, yet pervasive, message is that the primary mission of higher education is to guarantee students' material wealth. And almost two-thirds of Americans have entered into this post-secondary formation experience.[13] This shift in messaging coincides with the rising tide of material ambition among young people in the church. And while it seems obvious, nothing in this rundown of material gain meshes with the missional goals of Jesus:

> After breakfast Jesus asked Simon Peter, "Simon son of John, do you love me more than these?" "Yes, Lord," Peter replied, "you know I love you." "Then feed my lambs," Jesus told him. Jesus repeated the question: "Simon son of John, do you love me?" "Yes, Lord," Peter said, "you know I love you." "Then take care of my sheep," Jesus said. A third time he asked him, "Simon son of John, do you love me?" Peter was hurt that Jesus asked the question a third time. He said, "Lord, you know everything. You know that I love you. Jesus said, "Then feed my sheep." (John 21:15–17)

On the surface, this interchange has nothing to do with the momentum of materialism, but dig deeper and we see Jesus repeatedly framing our love for Him as other-centered giving ("Feed my sheep"). Our mission in life is to meet the needs of others—to "feed" their body, soul, heart, and mind—not feed our own material wealth in pursuit of the American Dream. If we love Him, says Jesus, then we'll naturally live out His heart in the world by attending to the needs of others as a priority. And that mission meshes well with the classic purpose of higher education: "Institutions of higher education should be aiming for more ideal contributions to the commonwealth society [than material gain]."[14] That's in sharp contrast to the marketing messages and promised outcomes of today's colleges and universities.

---

3. A Discipleship Infected by the Shadow-Theology of the Western Success Narrative—The core of discipleship, as spotlighted by Jesus, is about a grand defeat, not an empowering success. Our spiritual transformation process, He says, is on display in nature—"Unless a grain of wheat is buried in the ground, dead to the world, it is never any more than a grain of wheat. But if it is buried, it sprouts and reproduces itself many times over" (John 12:24 MSG). The path to growth in our relationship with Jesus always leads to a grave—as ominous as that sounds. "Dead to the world" is the way-station we must pass through on our way to flourishing. There, "buried in the ground," the grain of wheat that is our identity transcends the common materialist success narratives that infect our lives. We let go of the empty "get more to be more" promises that tamp down our soul—the vaporous pursuits that ensure we'll never be "more than a grain of wheat." Jesus is telling us the truth about the path to flourishing, but we don't easily stray from the road most traveled—the way of the Western Success Narrative.

> The core of discipleship, as spotlighted by Jesus, is about a grand defeat, not an empowering success.

In the West, we've been told that life is about summiting mountaintops, not descending into valleys. We conflate the trappings of culturally defined success (primarily financial achievement) with the mission of Jesus in our life, polluting our worship and misinterpreting our salvation. Because we've been taught to avoid walking in valleys, we miss the experience of His transformational presence in the dark. As we pick our way through the "darkest valley," we discover Him walking with us: "I will not be afraid, for you are close beside me" (Ps. 23:4 NASB).

In *The Sound of Music*, a confused Maria needs the wise counsel of her Reverend Mother to discern which path she should take—the cloistered life of a nun or the "outside" life of a wife and mother. The answer: "Climb every mountain, ford every stream, follow every rainbow, 'til you find your dream." Conspicuously absent, of course: "Descend every grave-path."

The shadow-theology of success that urges us to climb every mountain leads us to an endless landscape of false summits, each one promising a wholeness that remains elusive. In a speech to the anti-materialist Anabaptist Hutterian Brethren, former US Senate Chaplain Richard Halverson said he could sense an impending "mighty visitation of God upon the Earth, upon the church." And when it happens, he predicted, "people in the evangelical community will have to move a lot more in the direction you [the Hutterians] are, more toward the simplicity, away from the materialism that I believe now has really infected badly the whole evangelical community."[15]

Halverson is referencing the coagulated motivations of a people who hope to grow as disciples of Jesus while simultaneously pursuing material abundance. Dr. Steve Farrrar captures this "spirit of the age" in a prayer that doubles as biting commentary on spiritual formation infected with materialism.

> Now I lay me down to sleep
> I pray my Cuisinart to keep
> I pray my stocks are on the rise
> And that my analyst is wise
> That all the wine I sip is white
> And that my hot tub is watertight
> That racquetball won't get too tough
> That all my sushi's fresh enough
> I pray my [smartphone] still works
> That my career won't lose its perks

My microwave won't radiate
My condo won't depreciate
I pray my health club doesn't close
And that my money market grows
If I go broke before I wake
I pray my Volvo they won't take.[16]

Jesus tells us it's possible to "gain the whole world but lose your own soul" (Matt. 16:26), but the reverse is also true—it's possible to "gain our soul *because* we lose the whole world." The endgame of death is resurrection; to be made new means we shed our caterpillar shell and discover we can fly. But a discipleship overtaken by the shadow-theology of materialism leads to toxic formation. "Human transformation at its core is learning to love the right thing in the right way," observes John Eldredge. "But instead of loving people and using things, we love things and use people."[17]

---

4. The Underlying Influence of Epicurean Philosophy in Western Culture—In the early 300s BC, the Greek philosopher Epicurus accidentally founded a movement that was later named after him—Epicureanism. Simply, Epicurus believed that pleasure was the "chief good in life," and that the mission of human beings is to squeeze as much pleasure as possible from our life circumstances. Typical of a Greek thinker, his original version of this philosophy elevated the pleasures of the mind over physical pleasures. Followers through the centuries have not made the same distinction. Epicurus thought it was important to inoculate people against their fears of mortality and moral oversight by the "gods," because "punishment and fear of punishment would cause a person disturbance and prevent them from being happy." This led Epicureans to embrace, at a minimum, agnosticism.

Fast-forward to contemporary Western culture, and the influence of Epicureanism has so saturated our secular worldview that it has spilled its banks, overflowing into our Christian worldview. Robert Hanrott, author and editor of the blogging site Epicurus Today, describes the revival of Epicureanism in mainstream culture, and those who have tacitly embraced its values.

- They reject the form and style of so-called modern "democracy," which has been corrupted by big business and big money. By and large they take little part, and often do not vote.
- In Europe, at least, they reject organized religion with its bricks, mortar, and salaried priests, and are trying to work out their own personal philosophies of life, sometimes based upon Christianity, sometimes not.
- The old family connections are in disrepair owing to divorce and social changes. The young now create their own Epicurean metaphorical "Gardens" among their closest friends, keep in daily touch with them by cellphone. They regard their friends as their family, just as Epicurus did.
- Most believe in Darwinism, in decent (as opposed to corrupt) science, and in moderation, a balanced life, and common sense.
- They increasingly resent and reject the pressures put upon them by the modern capitalist system, and are finding ways of opting out or pushing back, reducing stress and anxiety. The high priests of capitalism have reason to fear the quiet rebellion emerging among younger people, who, given a choice between a calm life and endless stress (for the benefit of absent and uncaring management), will increasingly choose tranquility.[18]

Most of these are apt descriptions of Millennial and Gen Z values and lifestyles—both outside and inside the church. In this contemporary Epicureanism, the sheep (not the Shepherd) are in charge of their own material happiness and success in life—the chief curators of their moral, social, and spiritual worlds. The sheep are generally grateful that there is such a thing as a Shepherd, as long as He never meddles with their self-determination. They see themselves as functionally autonomous until they encounter a trouble they can't escape. And because the sheep are in charge of their own shepherding, they guard their autonomy by advocating for every other sheep's autonomy. This is the path to peace. As Paul writes to Timothy, the sheep have come to "love pleasure rather than God. They will act religious, but they will reject the power that could make them godly" (2 Tim. 3:4–5).

In a Barna study of Christians and competing worldviews, almost two-thirds of people who identify as followers of Jesus today embrace a value system rooted in New Spirituality, infecting the church with a palatable version of Epicureanism (Millennials and Gen Z believers are even more invested). This means they believe, for example:

- "All people pray to the same god or spirit, no matter what name they use for that spiritual being." *(You do you, and I'll do me—that's how we keep the peace.)*
- "Meaning and purpose come from becoming one with all that is." *(There is no locus of worship or obedience in my life—meaning is derived only from what I find meaningful in my sphere of experience.)*
- "If you do good, you will receive good, and if you do bad, you will receive bad." *(The concept of grace is offensive, because it violates my self-determination, or my agency over my own happiness.)*
- "God helps those who help themselves."[19] *(I'm the engine that drives the transmission of goodness in my life, and God exists only to add momentum to my autonomously chosen efforts.)*

Epicureanism offers material pleasure as our ticket to a life "free of fear." In contrast, according to "the disciple Jesus loves," freedom from fear is the natural fruit of our intimacy with Jesus. "God is love," writes John in his epistle, "and all who live in love live in God, and God lives in them. And as we live in God, our love grows more perfect. . . . Such love has no fear, because perfect love expels all fear. If we are afraid, it is for fear of punishment, and this shows that we have not fully experienced his perfect love" (1 John 4:16–18). King David would agree: "You are my Master! Every good thing I have comes from you. . . . Troubles multiply for those who chase after other gods. I will not take part in their sacrifices of blood or even speak the names of their gods. LORD, you alone are my inheritance, my cup of blessing. You guard all that is mine" (Ps. 16:2–5).

The Infiltration of Cancerous Greed

Wendell Berry, in his essay "A Native Hill," says:

> We have lived by the assumption that what was good for us would be
> good for the world. And this has been based on the even flimsier as-
> sumption that we could know with any certainty what was good even
> for us. We have fulfilled the danger of this by making our personal
> pride and greed the standard of our behavior toward the world—to
> the incalculable disadvantage of the world and every living thing in
> it. And now, perhaps very close to too late, our great error has become
> clear. It is not only our own creativity—our own capacity for life—that
> is stifled by our arrogant assumption; the creation itself is stifled.[20]

Berry's diagnosis of a cancerous belief infiltrating our assumptions
about a well-lived life, that "personal pride and greed" are somehow
"good for the world," meshes well with writer Kyle Roberts's observations:
"The gospel of grace contains no promises of preservation from harm—
or that you'll acquire material wealth or comfort. But the message communicated by the conflation of nationalism and Christianity is that prosperity, opportunity, and security are by-products of God's blessing on our
nation. That's not the gospel."[21]

It's this corruption of the gospel that Jesus targets in the parable of
the rich man and Lazarus (Luke 16:19–31). In the parable, Jesus describes
a "certain rich man" as "splendidly clothed in purple and fine linen and
who lived each day in luxury." At the rich man's gate lay a poor, sick, and
dying man named Lazarus, "longing for scraps from the rich man's table"
and unable to fend off the dogs who "would come and lick his open sores."
After both men die, Lazarus ascends to heaven, where he's given a place of
honor next to Abraham. The rich man, however, descends to "the place of
the dead," where he is tormented by flames and thirst. When the rich man
pleads for comfort, Abraham points out that he has already experienced
all the comfort he's going to get while he was alive, and the chasm separating him from Lazarus is too wide to cross. Though the rich man begs and

pleads for relief, even asking for mercy on behalf of his still-living brothers, Abraham is unmoved: "Moses and the prophets have warned them. Your brothers can read what they wrote."

In crafting this story, a tough-love Jesus is intent on bankrupting our golden-calf defaults—those who invest themselves in material salvation will, by definition, lose all of that investment when they physically die. The body can no longer reap the benefits of material gain when it transitions into a lifeless shell. But those who invest in the immaterial—in an intimate and trustful dependency on the God we cannot see—receive back a comfort that can never be taken away and will never expire. This story is an unmistakable and sharp-edged correction to our sheepy addiction to materialism as a false god. And, it's important to remember, the Good Shepherd (however stern He seems at times) always has the best interests of His sheep at heart.

Pastor and author David Platt offers an exclamation mark: "This is the picture of Jesus in the gospel. He is something—someone—worth losing everything for. And if we walk away from the Jesus of the gospel, we walk away from eternal riches. The cost of nondiscipleship is profoundly greater for us than the cost of discipleship. For when we abandon the trinkets of this world and respond to the radical invitation of Jesus, we discover the infinite treasure of knowing and experiencing him."[22]

Walking the Way of (the Unedited) Jesus

What will it look like if we walk in the way of the unedited Jesus, decoupling ourselves from material salvation while still working diligently to provide for our families? And what might happen when our eyes are opened to the beauty of His heart, a "treasure hidden in the field" that makes all other treasures seem like expendable trinkets? It will look like we have found freedom from material captivity.

The apostle Paul says: "I have learned how to be content with whatever I have. I know how to live on almost nothing or with everything. I have learned the secret of living in every situation, whether it is with a full stomach or empty, with plenty or little. For I can do everything through Christ, who gives me strength" (Phil. 4:11–13). Paul is describing a kind of freedom most in Western society can't imagine. To "live on almost nothing" is the definition of defeat and despair, not strength and hope. But the deeper challenge in Paul's revelation is that he is also content when he has plenty of "everything."

He is not proposing a set of practices that lead to material-freedom; he is urging a way of living that elevates the Spirit's influence and guidance over our material life. And he has *learned* this way of living—just as we can learn it. Paul's life practice is to continuously reinvest his hope and dependence in Jesus. Put another way, he trusts his Shepherd, not himself, to take care of him. His "secret" is simple—whether he has a lot or a little, he focuses his trust on his relationship with Jesus, not his own assets. "Everything else is worthless when compared with the infinite value of knowing Christ Jesus my Lord. For his sake I have discarded everything else, counting it all as garbage, so that I could gain Christ and become one with him" (Phil. 3:8–9).

Because Paul intends to nurture a great love that overshadows all other loves, it doesn't really matter to him whether he is materially rich or poor. There's a pivotal scene in the film *Jerry and Marge Go Large*, based on the true story of a Michigan couple (Jerry and Marge Selbee) who discover a flaw in the state lottery and realize they can beat the odds, rescuing their little town from oblivion by amassing $26 million in winnings. When Tyler, a Harvard student who's discovered the same flaw, threatens to use his computer hacking skills to destroy their lives unless the couple drops out of the scheme, Jerry backs down. The prospect of losing everything they've gained frightens him. But then Marge delivers a Pauline challenge to Jerry: "Well, you've calculated Tyler's threat, and the value of the game. But binomial distribution doesn't consider the third factor. That as long as we have each other, we are not afraid to be stupid."[23] In this context, "stupid" means that a great love makes the risk less . . . risky. If they lose everything, but still have their love, they win. If they gain everything, but still have their love, they win.

When we, like Paul, "count everything else as garbage" so that we can "become one with Jesus," we are not afraid to be "stupid" about our material needs. So, when we have little, we are not afraid to trust Jesus to care for us: "Look at the birds. They don't plant or harvest or store food in barns, for your heavenly Father feeds them. And aren't you far more valuable to him than they are?" (Matt. 6:26). And when we have much, we are not afraid to trust Jesus *beyond* our material resources: "Wherever your treasure is, there the desires of your heart will also be" (Matt. 6:21). The writer of Hebrews sums it up: "Don't love money; be satisfied with what you have. For God has said, 'I will never fail you. I will never abandon you'" (Heb. 13:5). As long as we have Jesus, we have the courage to "stupidly" trust Him in the face of our life circumstances, whether we are rich or poor.

The key to this kind of material freedom is, simply, experiencing the "greater treasure" of Jesus Himself. Once we "taste and see" the goodness and beauty in the heart of Jesus, we do whatever it takes to grow in an intimate relationship with Him—it happens naturally. This is the obvious point of the two micro-parables Jesus tells about a treasure hidden in a field and a pearl of great price in Matthew 13. It's perfectly reasonable to give up something of comparatively low value to acquire something of inestimable value. If we comprehend the value of the pearl and the treasure, we'll give up everything to get them. The unedited Jesus is not *shoulding* us to tamp down our material obsessions; He's inviting us to "taste and see" His goodness and beauty, then treasure Him above them. To *should* is to force a change in our behavior; instead, Jesus wants us to freely choose that path because we have comprehended the beauty of a greater treasure and are determined to pursue it.

And so, we take our first steps into appreciating the greater treasure of Jesus, and releasing ourselves from the grip of materialism by slowing down and paying ridiculous attention to His heart—so we can properly value the treasure that He is.

Let's revisit the Good Shepherd's warning about investing our heart in things that are, by definition, temporary (whether it's happiness or material gain): "Don't store up treasures here on earth, where moths eat them and rust destroys them, and where thieves break in and steal. Store your treasures in heaven, where moths and rust cannot destroy, and thieves do not break in and steal" (Matt. 6:19–20). C. S. Lewis, writing in *Mere*

Christianity, points the way to the storehouse:

> Give up yourself, and you will find your real self. Lose your life and
> you will save it. Submit to death, death of your ambitions and favor-
> ite wishes every day and death of your whole body in the end: sub-
> mit with every fibre of your being, and you will find eternal life. Keep
> back nothing. Nothing that you have not given away will ever be really
> yours. Nothing in you that has not died will ever be raised from the
> dead. Look for yourself, and you will find in the long run only hatred,
> loneliness, despair, rage, ruin, and decay. But look for Christ, and you
> will find Him, and with Him everything else thrown in.[24]

Reflection/Discussion Questions for Individuals or Small Groups

The Golden-Calfing of Materialism

- If you assess your own relationship with materialism, has it had a strong, medium, or weak influence on your choices and pursuits in life? Explain.

- How has the promise of the "American Dream" had a positive impact in our culture? Negative impact?

- In what ways has your participation on social media impacted your feelings of "personal relative deprivation"?

- How you seen this John Eldredge quote proven true in your experience: "Instead of loving people and using things, we love things and use people"?

- How have you seen and experienced the emptiness of materialism's promises in your life?

- There are no "rules" about how much is "okay" to acquire or achieve—so what does it mean to live counter to the pressures of materialism?

- If you had been present when Jesus told His parable of the rich man and Lazarus, what's one question you'd ask Him? What do you know about the heart of Jesus from this parable?

- To what degree have you "learned how to be content with whatever [you] have"? And what has helped you to grow in this?

- Paul says he "counts everything else as garbage" in comparison to knowing and following Jesus—what do you think he means?

6

The Dismissing of the Supernatural

***

"The blind see, the lame walk, those with leprosy are cured, the deaf hear, the dead are raised to life, and the Good News is being preached to the poor."
MATTHEW 11:5

Well-known Jesus skeptic, self-proclaimed "agnostic atheist," and University of North Carolina professor of religious studies Dr. Bart Ehrman, in a project for the History Channel, says this about the role of the supernatural in Christian history:

> Miraculous powers were the Christians' evangelistic calling card, their compelling proof. Jesus himself, the son of God, had performed one miracle after the other. He was born of a virgin; he fulfilled prophecies spoken centuries earlier by ancient seers; he healed the sick; he cast out demons; he raised the dead. And if all that wasn't enough, at the end of his life he himself rose from the grave and ascended to heaven to dwell with God forevermore. His disciples also did miracles—amazing

miracles—all recorded for posterity in writings widely available. And the miracles continued to the present day. People became convinced by these stories. Not en masse, but one person at a time.[1]

It's a strange observation, because Ehrman remains personally unconvinced that Jesus is divine and that Christianity is true. But he's exploring the way the Christian gospel spread so quickly and broadly throughout the ancient world, and it's impossible to sidestep the obvious: *the supernatural "signs and wonders" that characterize Jesus and His followers are key to the rapid and profound impact of the faith.*

As people are healed of incurable medical conditions and raised from the dead, the world pays attention. Never before has anyone seen a basket of food multiplied to feed a crowd of thousands, or a man strolling through the waves on a stormy sea, or the water in enormous earthen jugs transformed into wine. Word spreads quickly because these strange stories won't stop coming—the four gospels record thirty-seven of Jesus' supernatural acts, and His close friend John says that's just a sampler: "Jesus also did many other things. If they were all written down, I suppose the whole world could not contain the books that would be written" (John 21:25).

Jesus uses His track record with supernatural acts as a sort of resume. When John the Baptist, through two of his disciples, asks Jesus, "Are you the one who is to come, or should we expect someone else?" Jesus responds counterintuitively by simply listing the miraculous things He does: "Go back and report to John what you have seen and heard: The blind receive sight, the lame walk, those who have leprosy are cleansed, the deaf hear, the dead are raised, and the good news is proclaimed to the poor" (Luke 7:19, 22 NIV). Jesus knows His cousin will understand this clear reference to Isaiah's prophetic markers for the coming Messiah: "And when he [the Messiah] comes, he will open the eyes of the blind and unplug the ears of the deaf. The lame will leap like a deer, and those who cannot speak will sing for joy!" (Isa. 35:5–6).

Jesus' proof-of-Messiah list, the "Work Experience" section of His resume, is impressive. But we know it has nothing to do with us—Jesus is describing what *He* has done, not what He expects *us* to do. Supernatural acts like these cannot be, should not be, a reasonable expectation for people who are merely following Jesus, not channeling Him.

Except that's not what Jesus explicitly tells His disciples.

The Signs-and-Wonders Lifestyle

Just after Jesus stuns them by commanding a dormant fig tree to wither on the spot, He doubles down with His amazed disciples: "I tell you the truth, if you have faith and don't doubt, you can do things like this and much more. You can even say to this mountain, 'May you be lifted up and thrown into the sea,' and it will happen. You can pray for anything, and if you have faith, you will receive it" (Matt. 21:21–22). Later He drops this bomb on them: "I tell you the truth, anyone who believes in me will do the same works I have done, and even greater works, because I am going to be with the Father" (John 14:12).

Jesus treats His supernatural bucket list as if it's also *their* supernatural bucket list. Because supernatural acts are natural for Him, He intends to normalize them for His disciples. And as incredulous as they are in this moment, gawking at the withered fig tree, they will soon be living a signs-and-wonders lifestyle. Already, Jesus has given them "power and authority to cast out all demons and to heal all diseases" (Luke 9:1). And after Jesus' ascension the disciples "receive power when the Holy Spirit comes upon [them]" (Acts 1:8). As Ehrman points out, they go on to heal the sick, raise the dead, and cast out demons—first in Jerusalem, and then to the whole world as they are sent out to plant new churches.

Of course, we have access to the same Spirit that is animating the disciples, with the same latent capacity for miracle-working. But that's a dangerous and dissonant admission. Unless we ignore Jesus' mountain-throwing challenge, we're accountable to it. And so we have constructed theological arguments that will give us permission to ignore. In *Miracles*, C. S. Lewis sets the stage: "I use the word Miracle to mean an interference with Nature by supernatural power. Unless there exists, in addition to Nature, something else which we may call the supernatural, there can be no miracles. Some people believe that nothing exists except Nature; I call these people

Naturalists. Others think that, besides Nature, there exists something else: I call them *Supernaturalists.*"[2]

In the church, naturalist presuppositions infect our theology. Though we accept low levels of "everyday" supernatural practices such as prayer or worship, only uneducated, science-denying people give great credence to significant supernatural intrusions into the natural order of things. Robert Funk, founder of the controversial Jesus Seminar, explains: "The notion that God interferes with the order of nature . . . is no longer credible. . . . Miracles . . . contradict the regularity of the order of the physical universe. . . . God does not interfere with the laws of nature. . . . The resurrection of Jesus did not involve the resuscitation of a corpse. Jesus did not rise from the dead, except perhaps in some metaphorical sense."[3]

While most Christians would disagree with Funk's take on the bodily resurrection of Jesus, they would tacitly agree with the rest of his argument:

- Emotional and psychological struggles all have a natural source (and, of course, many often do).
- "Miraculous" healings are always the result of unforeseen biological processes or the "luck of the draw" (and sometimes they are).
- "Supernatural" encounters are universally the result of simple coincidence (and that's often true).

It's the *exclusion* of supernatural possibilities that marks our departure from the example and teaching of Jesus. Scott Bessenecker, Director of Global Engagement and Justice for InterVarsity, says: "Regarding our fixation with the material world, Western Christianity has nearly discarded the unseen world, pressing the faith into the shape of intellectualism and scientific theory. That's not to say that God's creation cannot be seen, measured, and understood from a material/scientific standpoint. It is simply to say that some in the West have written off dreams, visions, and unseen realities as mindless superstition."[4]

The Jesus who can't stop producing signs and wonders is trapped in the pages of our Bible, not free to show up in our everyday life.

Because we are both skeptical and uncomfortable with the "norming" of the miraculous, we have constructed a Christian life, and thus a Jesus, that is nearly devoid of it. The Jesus who can't stop producing signs and wonders is trapped in the pages of our Bible, not free to show up in our everyday life. Metaphorically, we have amputated the miraculous from the body of Christ—quite a feat, actually. Lewis observes: "One is very often asked at present whether we could not have a Christianity stripped, or, as people who ask it say, 'freed' from its miraculous elements, a Christianity with the miraculous elements suppressed. Now, it seems to me that precisely the one religion in the world, or, at least, the only one I know, with which you could not do that is Christianity."[5] Even so, we have found a way to engineer that impossible suppression . . . almost.

Our Relationship with the Supernatural-ly

Because we are made in the image of God, an affinity for the supernatural is hardwired in us—we can't completely tamp down our appetite for the miraculous. In addition to our everyday spiritual practices, we are fascinated by the paranormal and casually accepting of quasi-supernatural beliefs.

- A quarter of Americans overall (24 percent) and almost a quarter of all Christians (22 percent) say they believe in reincarnation—"that people will be reborn in this world again and again."
- Similar numbers (25 percent of the public overall, 23 percent of Christians) believe in astrology.
- And a third of Americans say they've felt a "real" connection with someone who's already died; almost a fifth say they've experienced ghosts.
- Meanwhile, the percentage of Americans who believe in psychics is creeping toward half (41 percent), and fully a third of the most committed Christians (32 percent) are in that camp.[6]

We seem well-primed to invite the kind of supernatural normalcy that characterized Jesus' life and ministry, and even to practice what He preached. Instead, when we consider His assertion—"You can pray for anything [and] you will receive it"—we treat it as either hyperbole or only meant for His first followers. So we push the mute button when He talks like this because His supernatural habits are cinematic. Like something from the Marvel universe, the accounts of His miracles are exciting, but outside the sphere of our reality. They are special effects woven into our favorite fairy tale.

According to a Pew Research project, a small percentage of Americans say they read Scripture daily (hovering around 10 percent), and only a fifth say religion is "*the single most important* source of meaning in their lives."[7] These are markers for *distance* in our relationship with God—the Jesus roaming our landscape is more of a rhetorical figure to most in the West, not a present Presence who's actually exercising supernatural agency in the world. So Jesus' normalized practice of the supernatural, and His expectations that we would share in that practice, have little traction in our everyday life. Maybe the charismatics and Pentecostals among us dabble in these realities, but not the majority who camp in the mainstream. We prefer to trust in our human capability— even the promise of "supernatural" human capability—over trusting in the present capabilities of Jesus flowing through us.

Duke sociologist Dr. Mark Chaves says: "It does strike me as interesting that belief in supernatural-ly kinds of things is more prevalent among the conventionally religious."[8] It's the "ly" Chaves adds to the end of "supernatural" that diverts attention away from God's agency and onto human agency. Our default temptation—the worship of lesser gods—entices us to explore our capabilities, even our supernatural-ly capabilities, outside of our dependence on God. Inside an intimate relationship with Jesus, where trust grows into something fundamental, signs and wonders have the potential to feel just as normal to us as they do to Him.

But relationships come with a steep price tag, and we usually prefer the bargain bin. "[People are] exploring alternative ways of being a spiritual being on a human path," observes psychotherapist Stephanie Anderson-Ladd, "as much as a human being on a spiritual path. We're open to many different ways to understand the divine."[9] Anderson-Ladd is spotlighting a default preference for human agency, outside of a relationship with God, in whatever we call "spiritual."

There is clear tension here between the exclusive claims of Jesus ("I am the way, the truth, and the life") and the nonexclusive expectations of "spiritual beings on a human path." If we're to be in relationship with Jesus, we have to account for His priorities and practices and norms. Outside of a relationship with Him, we can construct our own mash-up of spiritual beliefs and edit as we go. This gives us the comforting belief that we are in charge of our life, and we have no "significant other" to consider as we make our choices.

But the unedited Jesus is unapologetic about the choice He is giving us—we can sideline Him and go our own way, even experiment with the power promised by the paranormal, but we will spend all we've gained from that transaction and still be left empty and desperate. Jesus wants to decompartmentalize the natural and the supernatural, and He wants us to find our source for both in our relationship with Him. And if that's going to happen, it will not depend on what Jesus is capable of doing, it will depend on what *we believe* He is capable of doing.

The Nazareth Effect

Over and over in the gospel accounts of His three-year ministry, Jesus goes out of His way to assign credit for the miraculous outcomes that mark His encounters with needy people—seven times He tells a healed person, "Your faith has made you well." He does not say, for example, *My power has made you well.* That's because His power is a constant, and not dependent on a shifting capacity for the supernatural. It's the faith of the needy people who seek Him out that makes the difference. And by "faith," I simply mean what Jesus meant—the childlike belief that He is who He says He is.

It's as if Jesus is comparing our faith to the knob on a faucet—His supernatural ability is the water supply, and our faith is the spigot that can be opened or stay closed. But to "open our spigot" we need to know Him more intimately, so we can trust Him with childlike acceptance. Everything in the kingdom of God is invitational. That means Jesus invites supernatural interventions, but never forces them. An invitation asks for a corresponding invitational response—a trusting "yes" to His outstretched hand.

This explains why epic miracles accompany Jesus everywhere He goes, except for one outlier:

> Jesus left that part of the country and returned with his disciples to Nazareth, his hometown. The next Sabbath he began teaching in the synagogue, and many who heard him were amazed. They asked, "Where did he get all this wisdom and the power to perform such miracles?" Then they scoffed, "He's just a carpenter, the son of Mary and the brother of James, Joseph, Judas, and Simon. And his sisters live right here among us." They were deeply offended and refused to believe in him. Then Jesus told them, "A prophet is honored everywhere except in his own hometown and among his relatives and his own family." And because of their unbelief, he couldn't do any miracles among them except to place his hands on a few sick people and heal them. And he was amazed at their unbelief. (Mark 6:1–6)

The reason other people in other places are healed, but not in Nazareth, is simple—His Nazarene neighbors and friends think they know Jesus, but they don't. The Jesus they see in front of them is just a carpenter's son, not the Son of God. They've heard about the signs and wonders He leaves in His wake, but He must have padded His resume. He needs to be taken down a notch. Their "unbelief" restrains Him from offering the supernatural help so many others have already experienced. His neighbors and friends are suffering from the arrogance of overfamiliarity. To resolve the dissonance between the Jesus they think they know and the Jesus who "amazes," they edit His "offensive" supernatural power and reduce Him to a pretty good teacher with a messiah complex.

We are also the overfamiliar friends and family of Jesus—just as the Nazarenes did, we edit His offensive supernatural power to fit our alternate version of mere Christianity, reducing Him to a pretty good teacher who did some pretty crazy things back in the day. We love His teachings (at least, the ones we agree with). We can appreciate His wisdom and presence from a distance. But the miracle-working Jesus is a bull in our china shop, and no reasonable person invites that kind of chaos into their protected spaces. Like the Nazarenes, overfamiliarity is our biggest threat. Jesus is not a new concept for us, so we explain away (or block out) His miracles; we don't invite Him to have actual power in our lives.

For a season of my life, I was involved in what might be best described as "deliverance" ministry. After college, I joined an international missionary training school to learn how to connect with people and talk to them about Jesus. I lived in Rome for three months during the program, then our team traveled south for three weeks on an outreach experience in Sicily. In the middle of an evangelistic event, a woman came screaming and flailing into our midst, apparently possessed by a demon. It was like something out of a movie. There were no experts in the room prepared to handle this. That meant my friends and I had to trust the Spirit of Jesus to show us what to do, right then. So we prayed and asked for help. Then we prayed over this woman as best we could (in English, a language she didn't understand), trusting Jesus to assert His authority over any oppressive spirits. The woman promptly stopped screaming and frothing and thrashing. She became calm, as if someone had flipped a switch inside her. We stood amazed at the power of God, and we were drawn more deeply into intimacy with Jesus through this highly charged and dependent experience.

Many years later, I met with a counselor who had a long track record of deliverance ministry. From him, I learned the theological foundations for engaging demonic presences, and the practical patterns and skills needed to help people find freedom from their captivity. I partnered with an experienced ministry friend to meet with people who felt locked in a struggle against demonic oppression. We listened, discerned, then prayed under the counsel of the Spirit. When we did, people found freedom. Sometimes it was apparent that the person had psychological or emotional issues best treated by medical intervention, not spiritual intervention. We are whole people—body, mind, and spirit—and we can find healing in all three arenas.

These "deliverance" encounters were always nondramatic and relaxed. This type of supernatural intervention involves simple authority, not emotional fireworks—this is why Jesus marveled at the centurion's understanding of authority as the lever that would bring healing to his dying servant (Matt. 8:9). To His disciples Jesus said: "I have been given all authority in heaven and on earth. Therefore, go and make disciples of all the nations" (Matt. 28:18–19). The Spirit of Jesus in us exercises ultimate authority over both the seen and unseen, even over the natural order of things.

In the midst of this season of the supernatural in my life, I drove a carload of ministry coworkers to a mountain retreat. I'd just prayed for deliverance for a tormented young man the day before, but had no intention of talking about it—I never shared these experiences with my friends. But for some reason, on that long drive, I let slip what had happened the previous afternoon. And it was like lightning struck the car. My friends were flabbergasted by my "secret" supernatural life. Nothing about my involvement with deliverance ministry seemed normal or reasonable or even possible. They had always thought of me as an orthodox, conventional person, but no more. I was now peculiar. And this is exactly why I never talked about this aspect of my life. Peter called the followers of Jesus "a peculiar people" (1 Peter 2:9 KJV)—it's not easy to own that description.

> **We either immerse ourselves too deeply in signs and wonders, or refrain from even dipping our toe in the water.**

But there is an obvious dissonance here. The supernatural marks Jesus' life, ministry, and death. He often confronted demonic presences, and specifically taught His disciples how to go about it. Even when there was no obvious need for a supernatural act (walking on water in the Sea of Galilee, for instance), He did it anyway. He's even playful about it—turning water into wine at a friend's wedding and paying the temple tax He owes by sending Peter out to the shoreline to catch a fish with a coin in its mouth. He is rarely intense or overserious about the supernatural experiences He catalyzes—and He intends that those who follow Him would have the same easy relationship with the miraculous. But we almost never do that—we either immerse ourselves too deeply in signs and wonders, or refrain from even dipping our toe in the water.

We can track these extremes back to the Enlightenment, which tried to rid the church of its belief in the supernatural, dropping a brick wall between the ways of Jesus and common Christian practice. Hegel scholar Dr. Jon Stewart, in his book *An Introduction to Hegel's Lectures on the Philosophy of Religion*, says: "The thinkers of the Enlightenment wanted merely to hold firm to what they regarded as rational, while purging religion of what they took to be superstitious, childish views without foundation."[10] Riding the wave set off by the naturalist philosophers, enlightened religious leaders set themselves to keep superstitious beliefs and practices from intruding into everyday life. For many in the church, that meant any supernatural belief or practice was under immediate suspicion. Those who resonated with this shift saw themselves as rationalists determined to mature the church out of its childishness. Those who clung to the old beliefs gravitated to extremes as they fought this new mentality.

These two camps are still clearly evident in contemporary church culture. But there is a middle way between the unrestrained overemphasis on the supernatural and the skeptical and cynical underemphasis on it. That way is the way of Jesus.

Walking the Way of (the Unedited) Jesus

What will it look like if we walk in the way of the unedited Jesus, opening ourselves to "normalized" supernatural interventions while remaining unimpressed by the overemotional fireworks that people assume must accompany them? Here's a menu of possible trust experiments:

---

1. Trust and respond to the Ryder Box inside us.

I have a favorite metaphor for trusting the guidance and power of the Spirit in our everyday life—it's the RydeSmart technology created by the Ryder rental truck company. Inside the cab of every Ryder truck sits a little box that tracks the truck's location, speed, and fuel efficiency, sending that information to a central monitoring hub. It can even read and report back on "check engine" lights. It's a system that gives the driver, and an overseer, real-time information to make informed decisions—like having a truck doctor on board who's continually diagnosing the patient and offering prescriptive help. The hub's overseer isn't driving the truck, and isn't distracted by the driver's circumstances—that means the help provided comes from a broader, better-informed, and targeted perspective.

Followers of Jesus who are, every day, leaning into a more trusting relationship with Him can learn to sense and respond to the Ryder Box inside, otherwise known as the Holy Spirit. As we do, we don't *work up* our willingness to invite the supernatural, as if it was under our control. We simply respond in obedience to what the Spirit of Jesus asks us to do, trusting in His power, not ours. This means we pay closer attention to knowing Him more deeply. And in knowing Him we see Him better, and in seeing Him better we trust in Him more deeply, and in trusting Him more deeply we align ourselves with Him, and in aligning ourselves with Him we live our lives in an atmosphere of sensitivity to His Spirit.

Learning to trust the guidance of the Spirit is an art, not a science—we move from a performance mentality to a posture of warm obedience. The catalyst for this movement is dependence. We consciously turn from trusting only our own sensibilities to inviting the Spirit's sensibilities to guide us. We listen with expectation. We believe, even if we're buffeted by unbelief. We act on our belief by taking baby steps to trust. When the results aren't what we expect, we don't take ourselves too seriously. It's much more like play than work. In fact, my friend (the same one who partnered with me to help free others from oppression) calls dependence on the Spirit "playing." The only difference between the Nazarenes (who refused to move past their preconceived expectations) and those who found healing from Jesus is their refusal to believe in His capabilities. When we accept those capabilities as true, we act boldly in a spirit of humility and childlike adventure.

2. Help for our unbelief.

In Mark 9, a desperate man brings his oppressed son to Jesus' disciples for healing. But they're unable to cast out the "evil spirit" that is keeping the boy from speaking. Jesus charges that those closest to Him—those who have seen what He can do, over and over—remain "faithless." They struggle to believe in His true nature, and that He has authority over both the natural and supernatural world. So Jesus asks the man to bring the boy to him. "How long has this been happening?" He asks. The man replies, "Since he was a little boy. The spirit often throws him into the fire or into water, trying to kill him. Have mercy on us and help us, if you can." And Jesus responds: "What do you mean, 'If I can'? Anything is possible if a person believes." And this honest, determined, and humble man cries out: "I do believe, but help me overcome my unbelief!" Then Jesus rebukes the spirit, commands it to leave, and the boy is released. Later, His disciples ask why they'd failed, and Jesus explains, "This kind can be cast out only by prayer" (Mark 9:21–29).

We can extract from this story two crucial truths:

Dependence is key. Like the disciples, when we rely on "technique" or formula in the realm of the supernatural, we're immediately out of our depth. When Jesus explains why the disciples' efforts didn't work, he points to prayer—they thought they could "work up" the strength and authority to cast out an evil spirit on their own, but forgot where that strength and authority comes from. Dependence and attachment allow us to access the vast resources of the kingdom of God. When we do, we recognize that we are simply the conduit for the power of God, not its source. We actively remember, "Only God is good." And as conduits, our only responsibility is to open ourselves and believe.

We need help for our unbelief. If faith can move mountains, then we need faith-helpers that will help us overcome our unbelief. I mean, we need stretching exercises to help build our trust. I've found the best way to stretch myself to trust Jesus for supernatural intervention and breakthrough is to "play" more. Translated, that means I try trust experiments that depend on His capabilities, not mine. For example, when I pray for people in need I always pray dependently. I never assume I know what to pray or how to pray. And I don't assume the person I'm praying for knows what they most need, either. I pause in silence and ask Jesus first for guidance, then trust that guidance by acting on it. Usually, I ask Him to give me a word, a phrase, a Scripture passage, or even a picture of something as a starting point. Once that bubbles to the surface, I ask Him for guidance on how to pray or intercede. Then I act on it. But, of course, this is an imprecise process. I've long known I need help in learning to trust Jesus for the "normal supernatural."

For example, as an experiment in trust, I simply ask for a prompt to go to a specific passage in Psalms, read what's there (in context), and ask Jesus how He wants to guide my prayers through that lens. Then I pray for the person (or for myself) using that guidance. It's astonishing how often I pray for people (or myself) in ways I'd never know to do, even if I asked them what they needed. The Spirit knows better what they need. I've been investing in this playful practice for years and have seen my ability to believe and trust the Spirit progressively grow. I'm no longer surprised by the supernatural interventions that result from this—worship is my primary response.

It's easy to default into a performance mentality when we step into supernatural practices, just as the disciples did. The desperate man whose boy was held captive by demonic forces understood what's needed—we do believe, but often not without great struggle. We need a little help to enter more deeply into belief. Before you pray or intervene on behalf of someone, return to one of the many stories of Jesus acting supernaturally. Simply remind yourself of what Jesus is capable of, then enter into prayer. Redirect your attention away from your own capabilities and onto Jesus' capabilities by quieting yourself before you pray or intervene—repeat, over and over, something like, "Have mercy on us, Lord Jesus" or "Jesus, I need you." Once your soul is paying better attention to Jesus than to your worries or anxieties or doubts, enter into prayer.

3. Don't do anything alone.

This seems obvious, but because of the excesses and extremes associated with people who've engaged the supernatural immaturely or even abusively, we need accountability. If you're going to pray for a miracle or intervene on behalf of someone who needs supernatural help, do it with a spiritually mature partner. When in doubt, check your direction and path forward with that partner. Give each other permission to regulate what's happening, and confirm or redirect a prayer trajectory. Mutually submit, in a spirit of humility. And don't forget, because we are integrated people who are both spiritual and physical, some needed interventions are biological (medicines and treatments) and some are soul-based (counselors and therapists). There is no hierarchy of healing here—physical help is just as important as spiritual help.

When Jesus sent His disciples out to "heal the sick, raise the dead, cure those with leprosy, and cast out demons" (Matt. 10:8), He first paired them up. We need the support, encouragement, faith, and accountability of our community as we "play" with normal, everyday supernatural interventions in our life. We're members of a Body, and that means we work best in mutual dependence.

At the close of this chapter, there's a lot of dissonance to account for. But so far, I haven't mentioned the elephant in the room—that we sometimes pray "in faith" for supernatural intervention and nothing happens, or nothing happens right away. I've prayed, many times, for people and situations that don't change the way I hoped they would in the moment. I've never talked to anyone involved in the "normal supernatural" that has a perfect track record. It's a mystery; but if we require perfection as a prerequisite to risk and intervene, then maybe our courage or maturity is lacking. Our faith is bold because we trust Jesus, not our outcomes.

Our faith is bold because we trust Jesus, not our outcomes.

We don't understand everything, but too often we have let our lack of understanding keep us from stretching our trust muscles. Jesus sent out His disciples to be conduits for His miracle-working power *before* they understood everything about Him. In fact, we have plenty of evidence that their understanding of Him grew slowly over time—meanwhile, He gave them a challenging mission that required trusting Him for supernatural intervention. Maturity is not tied to our performance standards, but to our willingness to offer ourselves as a conduit for God's love.

It's good to remember this wisdom from Vineyard founder John Wimber: "The test of spiritual maturity is not the ability to speak in tongues, prophesy, or memorize Scripture. It's the ability to love God and others. Learning to serve others by loving the unlovely, the less fortunate, the lost, and the broken. This is the highest call, that we would fulfill our purpose on earth."[11]

The Dismissing of the Supernatural

- Jesus said, "I tell you the truth, if you have faith and don't doubt, you can do things like this and much more"—what does it mean to "have faith and don't doubt"?

- On the continuum between "naturalism" (nothing exists but nature) and "supernaturalism" (something beyond nature exists), where do you put yourself, and why?

- Why do we seem generally open to the possibilities of the paranormal, but skeptical and averse to the reality of the supernatural?

- How have you seen "the Nazareth Effect" influencing your relationship with Jesus—an overfamiliarity with Him that impacts what you believe He can do?

- What experiences have you had in life that seem supernaturally influenced, and why do you describe them that way?

- Why does Jesus do supernatural things when there's no real need for Him to do them?

- If you were trying to help someone grow to trust the guidance of the Spirit more deeply, what advice would you give, and why?

- What has helped you to grow in your belief of the supernatural power of Jesus?

- What's been your biggest hurdle to overcome in your openness to supernatural intervention in your life and the lives of others?

The Siren Song of Platforming

***

"Those who exalt themselves will be humbled, and those who humble themselves will be exalted."
MATTHEW 23:12

I've been an author for more than a quarter-century—on average, every other year I've published a new work. Writing books is both challenging and deeply satisfying. And because the focus of my work is always Jesus, it's also been an essential spiritual practice in my life, deepening my relationship with Him.

But in the last decade, I've felt a mounting pressure to develop my "personal brand" as a necessary platform for connecting with readers and, well, selling books. All authors now face this same hurdle—we are responsible not just for conceiving, producing, and shepherding each new work, but for embodying the work online and on social media. We are both the producers and the sellers. If you are not building your "platform" in this new reality, say publishing experts, you won't be a published author for long. And the most successful authors often have a broad social media footprint.

This promotional strategy is called platforming, and I've had an adversarial relationship with it. Self-promotion and personal branding aren't exactly the best ecosystems for growing other-centered maturity. I do interviews on podcasts and radio programs, write blogs, and occasionally post to two social media sites, but most experts in this field say that's the equivalent of first gear. Aggressive and persistent self-narrating on Twitter, Facebook, Instagram, YouTube, and TikTok is the standard. To counter this pressure, I remember Solomon's advice: "Guard your heart above all else, for it determines the course of your life" (Prov. 4:23). When I'm aggressively promoting myself my heart isn't right, and that toxic pollution flows downstream in my life. So I have to determine what level of engagement maintains my heart's integrity, and focus on relationship-building instead of platform-building.

Experts in platforming recognize that many have a hard time getting past their revulsion for self-promotion, but they insist that it's merely a means to an end—getting your message out to as many people as you can. Christian writer Jeff Goins, a well-known platforming apologist, explains its premise: "Whatever you want to do in the world, you need influence to make your voice count. Even a homemaker or schoolteacher needs authority to lead. And that has to come from somewhere, right? In the simplest terms, a platform is permission. It's the right to speak to a group about a certain topic. And there's nothing necessarily wrong with wanting that. If you have something worth saying, you want people to hear it. A platform amplifies and legitimizes your message. It gives you authority to influence."[1]

The message is subtle but clear—if what you have is worthy, you need the amplification and legitimizing influence of a bigger stage to make it count for something. Greater numbers equate to greater significance. This is the American way. So, how can I experience the true measure of my impact if my circle of influence remains small—or if praise and prosperity remain elusive? Without the expanding influence a platform provides, so the premise goes:

- My voice does not "count"
- My authority is unrecognized
- I lack permission to live out who I am
- My meaning and purpose is suspect

Platforming is not a practice reserved for authors and artists, of course. We all want our life and work to matter, and if platforming will help us get there, then the ends will have to justify the means. Self-promotion today is so widely accepted as a normal part of life that "build your own brand" is now a tired cliché. Twenty-five years ago, management guru and author Tom Peters was one of the first to predict and embrace this me-centered future: "We are CEOs of our own companies: Me Inc. To be in business today, our most important job is to be head marketer for the brand called You."[2]

Social media influencers and celebrities long ago jumped on this bandwagon, curating their personas to maximize their reach and opportunities. But the platforming/branding mindset has had a viral impact throughout the whole culture. Why work so hard to further the corporate goals of a company's brand when you can invest the same effort and creativity in furthering your own? For some, this means finding ways to monetize your identity—who you are is inextricably linked to what you earn. *New York Times* business reporter Emma Goldberg writes: "With personal branding, the line between who people are and what they do disappears. Everything is content; every like, follow, and comment is a professional boost."[3] When our "brand" is who we are, we become the product. And when people don't want to buy what we're promoting, it's shattering. It's dangerous to make ourselves the product we're in charge of selling—but that is the premise of personal branding on social media.

Social psychologist and professor Jonathan Haidt tracks the viral dynamics introduced a decade ago on our "Me Inc" timeline: "By 2013, social media had become a new game, with dynamics unlike those in 2008. If you were skillful or lucky, you might create a post that would 'go viral' and make you 'internet famous' for a few days. If you blundered, you could find yourself buried in hateful comments. Your posts rode to fame or ignominy based on the clicks of thousands of strangers, and you in turn contributed thousands of clicks to the game."[4] Haidt is saying the platforming ethic has a powerful forming influence on all of us, not just influencers. Today, almost five billion people are on at least one social media platform—that's two-thirds of the world's population.[5] The way we present ourselves in these spaces, and the attention that presentation attracts, shapes our identity.

The Medium Shaping the Message

The twentieth-century media philosopher Marshall McLuhan famously said: "The medium is the message." He meant that the conduits we use for communication reshape (and overtake) the message we're delivering. If that message is our own identity, then the tools of platforming (our common medium) will form us. This formation process is often at odds with our character formation, and it's in tension with the norms and values of the kingdom-of-God culture Jesus came to plant in our hearts.

In our hunger for meaning and purpose in life, it's difficult to resist the lure of the "personal branding promise." Do we really "need influence to make our voice count," or a persona-brand that "legitimizes our message"? For many in the Western Christian community, the answer is a disturbing "yes." In the 1950s, a scant 12 percent of US college students described themselves as "an important person," but the same study tracking that number over the decades pegs it at 80 percent three decades later.[6]

Of course, we are all "important" to the Jesus who leaves the ninety-nine sheep safe on a hillside to go after the one who is in need (Luke 15:1–7). Maybe 80 percent of us feel important because we've experienced mass healing of our self-esteem. But this migration in our collective identity, from common humility to common self-importance, is in conflict with the Jesus who says, repeatedly, "You must lose your life to find it." Meta-narcissism is fundamentally incompatible with life in the kingdom of God. And it has a cancerous impact on our soul—in a CDC report highlighting the steep decline in mental health among young people, experts track the downturn back to the rise of selfie culture, around 2012.[7]

While His disciples expect Jesus to pursue their default expectations of a Messiah—platforming His way to authority, power, and influence—Jesus intentionally avoids this path. In John 6, when "a huge crowd kept following him wherever he went, because they saw his miraculous signs as he healed the sick," Jesus purposely dismantles His platform after He crosses the Sea of Galilee to Capernaum. Eleven times in twenty-five verses, Jesus tells the gathered crowd, already rabid for what He has to give, that they need to eat His body and drink His blood if they want to continue to follow Him. When the confused and disoriented masses ask what He means, Jesus doesn't explain Himself. Instead, He repeats Himself, over and over. And in the end, the entire crowd, likely ten thousand people, desert Him in anger. Only His handful of close disciples are left, and Jesus asks, "Are you also going to leave?"

> **While His disciples expect Jesus to pursue their default expectations of a Messiah—platforming His way to authority, power, and influence—Jesus intentionally avoids this path.**

It would be hard to concoct a strategy that is more diametrically opposed to platforming than this one. And it's all on purpose; Jesus is intent on undermining His followers' expectations of conventional influence and impact in the world. He is planting the kingdom of God on earth, but not in the way we typically expect to catalyze a movement.

In what is now called the "2023 Asbury Awakening," students at Kentucky's Asbury University lingered in the school's chapel one February day after a normal weekly service to pray and worship. Somehow this mustard seed grew into a tree, almost overnight—scores of students joined those first few in the chapel, praying and worshiping twenty-four hours a day for more than two weeks. News of this "outpouring of the Spirit" spread around the world, with more than a hundred thousand people making a pilgrimage to Asbury to join the experience. When 24/7 Prayer founder Pete Greig arrived, he found an anti-platforming determination in the students:

I had the privilege of meeting with the leaders who are at the heart of this thing. . . . People think of this as a leader-less thing—it's not, it's being very strongly led. But it's being led by humble leaders. And we are so used to narcissistic leaders that when we see humble leadership we assume there's no leadership. . . . Inside [the chapel] is just this very gentle analog experience. . . . A very loving, gentle atmosphere. The guys leading worship are making it up as they go along, they'll sing one song for a half an hour. There's no words on the screen, there are zero production values. But the sense of the Spirit of the Lord is strong in there. . . . With no advertising other than organic social media. . . . There's no hype . . .

Everything that we think is necessary to gather a crowd is not happening, it is breaking all the rules. One of the leaders said . . . "The only celebrity is Jesus." Fox News wanted to come and film, and [the student leaders] said "no." And the anchorman on Fox News actually said, "Fair play." He said: "You have no idea how rare it is to find anything in the modern world that doesn't want TV cameras. When people don't want TV cameras there's only two reasons—mostly, it's because they're trying to hide something. But very occasionally it's because they just don't need the TV cameras. And what we've got here is something that doesn't seem to need the TV cameras."[8]

Humility stands out in a culture that is defined by normalized narcissism—that's why a student-led movement that refuses to cave in to the pressure of platforming inspires something like awe. We are weary of the preening that defines our culture, and when we encounter people who are not beholden to personal branding, it feels like a long drink of mountain-spring water. Fresh. Bracing. Thirst-quenching. It's no surprise that the meek and lowly attract the Spirit of Jesus, not the brazen and branded. "Learn from Me," He says, "for I am gentle and lowly in heart" (Matt. 11:29 NKJV).

Jesus is often among people drawn from every strata of ancient culture—the rich, the poor, and everything in between. But when He wants to retreat and restore His soul, He never gravitates to those who are invested in their own platform. Instead, His best friends are nobodies who are content to stay that way—they are filled up by their close proximity to the beauty of the unedited Jesus, not by the notoriety they can siphon from Him.

Our Siren Song

Though we recognize an attractive purity in movements like the Asbury Awakening, the lure of the platform mentality remains our "siren song"—a deception with destructive intent that is so intermingled with luring beauty that it is hard for us to resist. In Homer's epic poem *Odyssey*, the Greek hero-king Odysseus is warned against exposing himself to the deceptively beautiful song of two monsters (sirens) pretending to be beautiful women, who lure unsuspecting sailors to their death with their mesmerizing voices. Though he is warned, Odysseus can't help himself. He escapes the sirens only because he insists his sailors use ropes to bind him to the mast.

A pastor, writing in a popular evangelical magazine, exposes her Odysseus complex: "One day I was complaining to God about the huge platform minister so-and-so has. I lamented, 'If I had a platform as big as hers, I could reach more people for You and call the church back to the place of prayer.' I didn't expect God to answer my tale of woe, but He did. 'Who gave her that platform?' He cut right to the chase. 'Well, You did, Lord,' I humbly replied. God has a way of encouraging and correcting all at the same time. 'Can I give *you* a platform?' He poignantly asked. 'Yes, Lord, of course. You can do anything.' What seemed like a mountain was turning into a miracle. Hope was welling up inside of me. Then God ended His part of our discourse with two, powerful words: 'Ask Me.'"[9]

This pastor's awkwardly self-centered prayer, and the lure of "Ask Me," is like a spiritual shell game—she believes notoriety and influence and significance are hidden under one of multiple shells manipulated and controlled by God. If she will simply ask Him to lift the right shell, the prize awaits. It's no surprise that God is reinterpreted as a willing character in this self-aggrandizing bit of theater. Yuval Levin, a senior fellow at the American Enterprise Institute, researches the relationship between fame and virtue. He's noticed a shift in the motivation of those who run for political office, and makes the case that this same shift has infiltrated all institutions, including the church:

> I came to think that what was really happening was a transformation of [political institutions] from a place people seek to come to in order to make laws and influence public policy, to a place that people come to in order to become prominent players in the theater of our culture war.... This was something that was happening in a lot of institutions. We had transformed our expectations of institutions from expecting them to form people we could trust, to expecting them to display and elevate people as individuals on a platform.... Over and over, you find that rather than be formative, these institutions became performative; rather than be molds, they became platforms.[10]

Jesus is well familiar with this way of thinking, because He "has been tempted in all things just as we are, yet without sin" (Heb. 4:15 NASB). Just after the start of His public ministry, He is traveling around Galilee as an itinerant rabbi, teaching and healing. But His brothers, in an interchange saturated in mockery and disdain, goad Him to add more fuel to the fire of His popularity: "[Jesus] wanted to stay out of Judea, where the Jewish leaders were plotting his death. But soon it was time for the Jewish Festival of Shelters, and Jesus' brothers said to him, 'Leave here and go to Judea, where your followers can see your miracles! You can't become famous if you hide like this! If you can do such wonderful things, show yourself to the world!' For even his brothers didn't believe in him" (John 7:1-5).

Because He is saying and doing things they resent, Jesus' brothers prod Him to out Himself as the fame-monger they believe He really is. But Jesus pushes back, ignoring their platform-bait: "Now is not the right time for me to go, but you can go anytime. The world can't hate you but it does hate me because I accuse it of doing evil. You go on. I'm not going to this festival, because my time has not yet come" (vv. 6-8).

Jesus has no intention of currying favor with the world—or the system of values and beliefs that underlie personal branding. He will not go to the festival under the terms His brothers have laid out. So He stays back in Galilee while they depart for Jerusalem. When they are long gone,

Jesus sets out for the festival in secret. He's intentionally hiding Himself from public view, eavesdropping as the crowds debate about whether He's a "good man" or a "fraud." And then, "midway through the festival, Jesus went up to the Temple and began to teach. The people were surprised when they heard him. 'How does he know so much when he hasn't been trained?' they asked" (John 7:14–15).

Yes, Jesus draws a crowd at the Temple, but He is not using the crowd for self-promotion. The Festival of Shelters is marked by two metaphorical rituals that are repeated every day: 1) a symbolic pouring of water from the Pool of Siloam at the Temple altar as a reminder that the hoped-for Messiah will immerse a parched people in the life-giving waters of salvation, and 2) the lighting of four huge oil-fed candelabras symbolizing the pillar of fire that led the Israelites out of the wilderness—again, a nod to the promise of the coming Messiah. So, on the last day of these rituals, Jesus reveals Himself by standing to teach at the Temple. And what does He teach about? "Anyone who is thirsty may come to me!" and "I am the light of the world." Far from building His platform, Jesus is announcing Himself as the Messiah-now-here—a declaration that will lead to His capture, torture, execution, and resurrection. Jesus' decision to step into a public spotlight is self-sacrificing, not self-aggrandizing. His chosen platform is Golgotha.

The crowd-mongering force of platforming promises to prop up and legitimize our identity. But Jesus intends to restore our broken identity in quite a different way—we freely give ourselves to Him, and He freely gives us back our whole self. We lose our life to find it. And when we live out this trade in everyday life, our deep desire to be known and seen and enjoyed slowly shifts—we wander from the path of platforming, seeking out a new path, one that Henri Nouwen describes in reference to leaders, but with application to everyone: "I am deeply convinced that the Christian leader of the future is called to be completely irrelevant and to stand in this world with nothing to offer but his or her own vulnerable self."[11] Our vulnerability makes us relevant, not our platform.

Walking the Way of (the Unedited) Jesus

What will it look like if we walk in the way of the unedited Jesus, awake to the forming influence of platforming and determined to, instead, "walk humbly with [our] God" (Mic. 6:8)? Some possible ways forward:

---

1. Invite your soul to live in a merciful ecosystem.

"Rudolph the Red-Nosed Reindeer" is a beloved Christmas song that morphed into a beloved animated special. Though we've ingested this iconic story into our Christmas mythology, the crux of the story is disturbing—we deserve to be abused and bullied until we can prove our worth, and *only then* will others value who we are. I call it the "Rudolph Heresy." It's the same underlying toxic belief system that characterizes platforming—if you have a "defect," you deserve to be ostracized, unless you find a way to show how your defects are actually "valuable" assets.

It's an epic story of conditional love. Like Rudolph, Jesus' friend Zacchaeus is a pariah among his peers: *All of the other [ancient Jews] used to laugh and call him names. They never let poor [Zacchaeus] join in any [community gatherings].* But Jesus invites Himself into close friendship with Zacchaeus *before* he cleans up his act and proves his usefulness. He extends to Zacchaeus a merciful ecosystem, inviting him to leave the captivity of conditional love and enter the promised land of unconditional love. When we acclimate to the prison walls of personal branding or performance-framing on social media, we have to prove our worth or be relegated to isolation. But we can accept Jesus' invitation to live in a more merciful ecosystem.

If your online surroundings feel toxic to your soul, and if you feel compelled to curate your persona to maintain acceptance, leave those prison walls behind. Start with a one-day fast from these platforms, then work your way up from there. When I set out to lose forty pounds several years ago, I committed to a month-long change in my diet. It worked, and I grew to love healthy foods. The first time I had pizza after I lost all the weight, it tasted delicious. But within minutes of my first slice, I felt sick to my stomach. Unhealthy foods, delicious as they were, no longer made me feel good. That's helped me, since then, to pare back from them. The same dynamic works with our online diet. Give your soul a break from social media spaces—fill the emptiness with actual relational contact. At the end of the break, enter into those spaces again, and let your soul's "sick response" guide you into a more permanent diet change.

---

2. Move from a selfie mindset to an other-ie mindset.

Katelyn Beaty says: "The right kind of fame arises from a life well-lived, not a brand well-cultivated."[12] And what is a "life well-lived"? Researchers Doris Baumann and Willibald Ruch, psychologists at the University of Zurich in Switzerland, set out to discover the factors that lead to a fulfilling life. They interviewed almost seven hundred people, searching for common threads among those who reported high life satisfaction. Their conclusion? "The good life is not a self-centered life. Helping others, passing on one's experiences, or making a difference in one's environment—which can happen on a small scale—provides people the feeling that their lives matter. The beauty of this concept is that one can make a positive difference in another person's life regardless of age or resources."[13]

This finding propels us to shift our attention away from platforming and onto the unedited Jesus, from a selfie mindset to an "other-ie" mindset in our life. The visual metaphor for this is simple—when we're about to take a selfie, turn the camera around and highlight others instead. Then think about this literal reversal as a template for every other "selfie-like" pursuit in our life:

- When we would typically post a self-narration, we honor the narrative beauty of others instead (For example: "During the winter, my friend Shelly volunteers to help freezing homeless people find warm shelter—my hero!").
- When we would typically volunteer our own story in a social setting, we pursue the beauty of others' stories instead—that means we ask more than one follow-up question, and dig deeper, when we're exploring another's story.

- When we would typically offer family members suggestions for Christmas or birthday gifts, we add to the list a specific gift to a needy population (Compassion.org and WorldVision.org have fantastic Christmas giving options).
- When we would typically be heads-down, phones-up people, we're heads-up, phones-down people—we look people in the eyes and invest ourselves to enjoy them.
- When we would typically take credit, we give credit instead.

---

3. Be a team player.

Denver Nuggets center Nikola Jokic, a Serbian native, is a multiple winner of the NBA Most Valuable Player award and an NBA Finals MVP. It's a head-scratcher for many basketball experts and fans, because Jokic doesn't fit the athletic, spotlight-friendly player that typifies an MVP. He's a team player who values assists and rebounds over his own scoring. He plays a position not known for great passers, but his passing skills are legendary. He's such an unselfish, self-deprecating, atypical NBA superstar that his unconventional style has prompted a backlash from some basketball commentators. His crime? He's too much of a team player.

Like Jokic, if we're going to disrupt and upend a platforming culture, we'll walk in the way of the unedited Jesus and elevate Team over Me Inc. This is what John the Baptist did so openly with his disciples: "You yourselves know how plainly I told you, 'I am not the Messiah. I am only here to prepare the way for him.' It is the bridegroom who marries the bride, and the bridegroom's friend is simply glad to stand with him and hear his vows. Therefore, I am filled with joy at his success. He must become greater and greater, and I must become less and less" (John 3:28–30).

John the Baptist's mission is to "prepare the way" for the Messiah, not to *be* the Messiah. He's introducing a new way of living to a culture that has, until now, revolved around the haves, ignoring the have-nots. The platformers command attention, not "the least of these." John is promoting the insurgent values and priorities of a foreign culture called the kingdom of God—a culture native to the Messiah. In that culture, joy is tied to "less and less," not "greater and greater." In basketball terms, John is focused on his team winning a championship, and he doesn't care about his own "stats." In fact, he finds more joy in watching those he loves succeed than in promoting his own achievements (which are impressive).

Likewise, life in the kingdom of God is a mutual admiration society, where everybody is an "aprecionado"—the word pastor and leadership coach Tom Melton invented to describe someone who appreciates beauty in others with the focus and delight of an aficionado. Love for the beauty we experience in others shifts our attention from self to team. In his sermon "The Weight of Glory," C. S. Lewis expands on the aprecionado life: "It is a serious thing to live in a society of possible gods and goddesses, to remember that the dullest and most uninteresting person you talk to may one day be a creature which, if you saw it now, you would be strongly tempted to worship. . . . It is with the awe and the circumspection proper to them, that we should conduct all our dealings with one another, all friendships, all loves, all play, all politics. There are no ordinary people. You have never talked to a mere mortal."[14]

It took three years for Jesus to plant the values and priorities of the kingdom of God in the souls of his "players." Shortly after he marks Peter as a leader, He's forced to make a course correction—the headstrong fisherman elevates himself above the team after Jesus explains the sacrifice He'll need to make on the cross: "But Peter took him aside and began to reprimand him for saying such things. 'Heaven forbid, Lord,' he said. 'This will never happen to you!' Jesus turned to Peter and said, 'Get away from me, Satan! You are a dangerous trap to me. You are seeing things merely from a human point of view, not from God's'" (Matt. 16:22–23). Peter is working his own agenda, ignoring what is necessary for Jesus to embrace: *It's about the team, Peter, not about you.* When James and John, the "sons of thunder," ask Jesus to spotlight their status among the disciples by promising them seats of honor in the kingdom of God, He knocks their knees out from under them: "My Father has prepared those places for the ones he has chosen" (Matt. 20:23). Over and over, the unedited Jesus redirects His disciples' away from Me Inc and toward Team.

It's clear that the seeds of this Team-first mindset, first planted by Jesus, grew into a defining passion among the disciples. Late in his life, the apostle

John is still living out this kingdom-of-God way of living. In his apostolic letter to Gaius, written from his exile on the island of Patmos to an early church leader, he's upset for the same reasons a basketball player like Nikola Jokic would be upset. Someone who represents Jesus is focused on his own glory, not the Team's goals. That person is Diotrephes, a promising young leader who can't resist the siren song of platforming. He's elevating his own ministry by thwarting the influence of other teachers. "Not only does he refuse to welcome the traveling teachers," writes John, "he also tells others not to help them. And when they do help, he puts them out of the church. Dear friend, don't let this bad example influence you. Follow only what is good. Remember that those who do good prove that they are God's children, and those who do evil prove that they do not know God" (3 John 10–11).

Like John and the other disciples, the way we learn to experience joy in the Team's success, more than our own individual platforming, is to spend time with Jesus, inviting His value system to infect us and submitting to His correction. The deeper we experience His unedited beauty, and recognize that same beauty in others we respect, the more we nurture the seeds of Team-first in our own soul.

4. Practice gratitude in your obscurity.

The Trinity Forum's Cheri Harder offers a thumbnail sketch of gratitude's enduring impact: "G. K. Chesterton claimed that 'thanks are the highest form of thought.' Cicero asserted that gratitude is not only the greatest of all the virtues, but the parent of all others. And Martin Luther called it 'the basic Christian attitude and the heart of the gospel,' while Jonathan Edwards listed it as 'the sign of true religion.' More recently, gratitude has been the focus of numerous psychological and even medical studies, which have found that gratitude can lower stress, improve one's immune function, enhance cardiovascular function, sharpen memory, deepen sleep, increase energy levels, boost reported happiness, increase productivity, and strengthen relationships."[15]

Gratitude has a "best of show" pedigree among the character virtues. Not listed, though, is gratitude's inherent ability to defuse our platforming temptations. It's simple moral physics—when we yield to the Spirit of

Jesus in us, we push out honor to others rather than pull it toward ourselves. We live as remembering people, recalling the goodness of God and others by honoring it. It's the same spiritual habit modeled by the psalmists, who wrote the word "remember" dozens of times throughout the Psalms (e.g., Pss. 20:7; 63:6; 77:11; 119:52).

To remember is to adjust our posture in life—from "I'm important" to "He's important." We lean into a practice embraced by Vineyard founder John Wimber: "I'll take the encouragement, but I'll pass the glory on."[16]

5. Sit at the wrong end of the table.

Earlier, I highlighted an awkward moment when Jesus called out the obvious platforming behavior of guests at a religious leader's social gathering:

> When Jesus noticed that all who had come to the dinner were trying to sit in the seats of honor near the head of the table, he gave them this advice: "When you are invited to a wedding feast, don't sit in the seat of honor. What if someone who is more distinguished than you has also been invited? The host will come and say, 'Give this person your seat.' Then you will be embarrassed, and you will have to take whatever seat is left at the foot of the table! Instead, take the lowest place at the foot of the table. Then when your host sees you, he will come and say, 'Friend, we have a better place for you!' Then you will be honored in front of all the other guests. For those who exalt themselves will be humbled, and those who humble themselves will be exalted." (Luke 14:7–11)

This is Jesus at His pragmatic best—He's not shaming these upwardly mobile dinner guests into humility, He's pointing out how practically flawed their behavior is. We cannot seize honor, it is bestowed—and not always fairly. In contrast to our natural inclinations to self-promote, He's suggesting we self-demote. For some, this represents permission to diminish and deprecate the glory of God planted in us. We say things like, "Thank you, but that's all God, not me." Well, that sounds humble, but it's also not true. It's never all-God or all-us—we are living out an intimate partnership, a mutually giving relationship, that blends God's agency and our agency into a beautiful, imperfect gift. He enjoys doing things *with* us, not merely *for* us. The humility Jesus is recommending does not require us to *diminish* who we are; it's a warning about *promoting* who we are. It's Rick Warren's iconic insight: "Humility is not thinking less of yourself; it is thinking of yourself less."[17]

I'm oversimplifying, but "sitting at the wrong end of the table" has translated to *faithfulness over fame, fortune, and status* in my life. As I grow in my appreciation for the heart of Jesus, I find myself less interested in the "places of honor" at the table. That's not heroic humility—it's a recognition that Jesus hangs out at the wrong end of the table, and I want to sit where He's sitting.

Mark Sayers, pastor of Melbourne's Red Church and host of the *Rebuilders* podcast, describes a season in his life and ministry that was overshadowed by exhaustion and a descent into bipolar disorder. His psychiatrist recommended quiet and rest. And then he got the upending news that he and his wife would soon have twins. One day, in the middle of his sermon, he became disoriented and walked off the stage and out of the church building. After such a public self-demotion, he was worried he'd no longer be welcomed or trusted in ministry. But, instead, his congregation responded with compassion and help—they elevated him. From this experience, Sayers learned what it means to sit at the wrong end of the table: "The way I had measured success was wrong," he says. "It wasn't about retweets, book sales, and buzz. It was about dying to self in public. It was not about building a career or a name. It was about operating out of complete dependency upon God. He was far more interested in what he wanted to do in me than in what I was doing. So I became focused on passing the baton to others, stepping out of the way so others could flourish."[18]

To sit at the wrong end of the table is to trust God as the source of our identity, not our platformed position. There is a deep security in this, because we are no longer beholden to our promotional skills—we can relax in our seat with other broken, imperfect, dependent people, none of us campaigning for seats of honor.

Lord Acton, the nineteenth-century historian, said: "Power tends to corrupt, and absolute power corrupts absolutely."[19] The corollary, relative to the pressure to adopt the Me Inc. mentality, is: "Platforming corrupts, and absolute platforming corrupts absolutely." For an extended object lesson in this truth, listen to *Christianity Today*'s much-acclaimed podcast series *The Rise and Fall of Mars Hill*, created and hosted by Mike Cosper. This painstakingly researched history lesson on the perils of platforming in Christian ministry is an unforgettable gut-punch—a reminder we sheepy people need as we navigate a culture that depends on our unwitting acceptance of personal branding as a no-victims way of life.

Reflection/Discussion Questions for Individuals or Small Groups

The Siren Song of Platforming

- How has the "platforming" mentality in our culture influenced you in your everyday life?

- If our influence is not tied to the size of our platform, then how do we gauge our impact?

- Why has the percentage of people who describe themselves as "an important person" skyrocketed over the decades?

- Why is Jesus so averse to, or so unconcerned about, "building His platform"?

- Why is Jesus so drawn to people who have no interest in building their platform?

- Yuval Levin says institutions like the church have become more "performative," rather than "formative"—why is that?

- In what ways have you tried to extract yourself from the platforming mentality prevalent in our culture, and what has been the outcome?

- How and why have you grown in a "Team-first" mentality in your life?

- In your life, what does it mean to "sit at the wrong end of the table"?

8

The
De-prioritizing
of Justice

✱ ✱ ✱

**"You are careful to tithe . . . but you ignore
justice and the love of God."**
LUKE 11:42

An interviewer asked International Justice Mission founder Gary Haugen why some corners of the church treat justice issues as a distraction from the "meat" of the gospel truth Jesus came to spread. Haugen's reply is revelatory:

> It would be hard to look at the biblical text and think that justice was a distraction, since of course, it says that justice and righteousness are the foundation of God's throne… Likewise, all over in Scripture, God's people are directed to follow Jesus and the Kingdom of God in the work of justice. Micah 6:8 says, "He has told you, O man, what is good and what the Lord requires of you, but to do justice, love mercy, and walk humbly with your God." Jesus, in Matthew 23, repeats the same three priorities when he talks about [how] the Pharisees have neglected the weightier matters of the law: justice, mercy, and faith. In all of these, the first item on the list of three is justice.

So one has to then inquire what exactly is one speaking to when they're feeling that way? Because I certainly grew up in a church environment where justice was not well understood, mostly because the biblical material was neglected. In the evangelical tradition that I grew up in, [they] neglected [this] biblical material for about a hundred years. . . . I would have heard a thousand sermons by the time I had finished high school, and I would never have heard a sermon about justice.[1]

Haugen makes a *de facto* case for the importance of justice and advocacy in the heart of God, but also exposes the church's habit of "neglecting" the primacy of advocating for others. Later in the interview, Haugen adds: "Everyone has some power and it's in relation to other people. So how are you using your power? Are you using it to love and to serve?"[2]

These are central questions for us, because they are central to the ways of Jesus. When we neglect justice, we edit Jesus.

We know Jesus has condensed life down to two pursuits: 1) love God with all our heart, mind, soul, and strength, and 2) love our neighbor as ourselves (Mark 12:30). The two are mutually dependent—we can't truly love God and *not* love our neighbor, and we can't truly love our neighbor without the love of God in us. So, since Jesus narrows all of our life down to these two imperatives, let's revisit the metaphor Jesus uses to describe their interplay.

When we love God with all that we are, we are like a branch grafted into a Vine, so intimately attached that the life of the Vine flows into our branch, producing fruit (John 15:1–8). That fruit is the "produce" of God's heart, with justice (as Haugen points out) as a primary "crop." This is the organic force behind "loving our neighbor as ourselves," and a clear outcome in the lives of those who are relationally attached to Jesus. An American Enterprise Institute study finds that almost half of religious Americans (45 percent) advocate for others by volunteering with an organization, while only 13 percent of nonreligious people do the same.[3] Nevertheless, almost two-thirds of Americans believe the church (meaning, religious Americans) contributes "nothing" or "not much" to solving important social problems—they're convinced that works of compassion and justice in their community would still happen even "if there were no people of faith or religious organizations to do them."[4] This means there's a distinct disconnect between the perceived justice-consciousness of the church and what its people are actually prompted to do in their everyday life:

- Two-thirds of active churchgoers contribute to the poor, compared to two-fifths of other Americans,[5]
- Six out of ten of the emergency shelter beds are maintained by religious providers—who also deliver many of the addiction, healthcare, education, and job services needed to help the homeless.[6]
- Local congregations provide 130,000 alcohol-recovery programs, 120,000 programs that assist the unemployed, and 26,000 programs to help people living with HIV/AIDS.[7]
- Finally, churches are the primary source for the volunteers needed to operate organizations like Habitat for Humanity, Meals on Wheels, food pantries, feeding programs, Big Brothers Big Sisters, the Red Cross, and other justice-focused charities.[8]

The fruit is obvious—people attached to the Vine have an organic desire to "love their neighbor as themselves." And because Jesus tells us, clearly, that we can identify a tree by its fruit (Matt. 7:16), those who don't "bear the fruit of justice" in their life might want to pay closer attention to their "attachment" to the Vine.

We can't compartmentalize, marginalize, or trivialize the primacy of justice in the heart of God. A heart that ignores or diminishes justice is not deeply attached, and therefore not conformed, to the heart of Jesus.

Justice vs. Fairness

Jesus said many hard things—some seem impossible, actually. And none harder than this: "You have heard the law that says, 'Love your neighbor' and hate your enemy. But I say, love your enemies! Pray for those who persecute you! In that way, you will be acting as true children of your Father in heaven. For he gives his sunlight to both the evil and the good, and he sends rain on the just and the unjust alike" (Matt. 5:43–45). So, what does this phrase—*In that way, you will be acting as true children of your*

Father in heaven—really mean? A "true child" reflects the value system and character of the parent, and "love your enemies" means God does not play favorites when it comes to basic human needs. Even evil people receive the grace of sunlight and rain, the building blocks of survival. In this way, Jesus is trying to help us let go of fairness as our guiding passion and practice justice instead.

A couple of years ago I led a group of two dozen young people in an immersive justice-vs.-fairness experience. I gave each person a toy blowgun and a pink, yellow, and green dart (tipped with suction cups). I formed three color-coded teams—the goal was to be the team with the most hits on the other teams. Just before I started the competition, I asked each person to rate themselves on their level of blowgun accuracy, on a scale of one to ten. All of the "seven or above" people had an advantage, so I took away their blowguns. And all of the six or below people had a disadvantage, so I gave some of them an extra dart that I took from the seven-or-above people. Then I "released the hounds" and the air was filled with colored darts. After the winning team was crowned, I asked three simple questions:

1) *Was this game fair?*
2) *Was it just?*
3) *What would've made it both fair and just?*

To get to the heart of these questions we revisited Jesus' "rain and sunshine" proclamation in Matthew 5:43–45. We explored the fundamental differences between treating people fairly, and treating people justly. We all acknowledged how fairness-conscious we are, and that the game violated that sensibility. As we wrestled with the three questions, I scribbled notes on a whiteboard from our conversation, then recorded the group's collective conclusions:

- *Fairness can be just, but justice doesn't have to be fair.*
- *Justice is unafraid to advantage the disadvantaged and disadvantage the advantaged.*
- *Jesus came to fulfill justice by re-standardizing fairness, infusing it with love and grace rather than the "letter of the law" the Pharisees demanded.*

- *The "currency" in the kingdom of God is justice, because grace and love are not fair. And grace and love are the foundation of justice.*
- *In other words, it is not necessarily just to be fair, but it is fair to be just.*

The Pharisees attract the ire of Jesus because they elevate a "fairness" form of justice that violates grace—they care more about the letter of the law than the spirit of the law. Pastor and apologist Timothy Keller says: "Self-righteous religion is always marked by insensitivity to issues of social justice, while true faith is marked by profound concern for the poor and marginalized."[9] In the synagogue on Sabbath, Jesus encounters a man with a withered hand (Matt. 12:9–14). Yes, the letter of the law says it's a day set apart for rest, but Jesus heals the man anyway, infuriating the religious leaders. It's unjust to leave a man to suffer because a law meant to bless God's people is "fairly" practiced. Justice is governed by grace, which is the fulfillment of the law and the essence of Jesus.

In an extensive, deeply sourced piece titled "The Dissenters Trying to Save Evangelicalism from Itself," award-winning *New York Times* columnist David Brooks explores the takeover of the evangelical movement by extremist forces and the emergence of a budding renewal, led by a host of prominent evangelical outliers. Though this is a deep dive into a particular strata of the church, much of what Brooks highlights has traction for all of the church. He argues that, central to the hope of renewal, we need a deeper embrace of justice and reconciliation as the core of Christian orthodoxy.

Brooks writes: "Many of these [evangelical] dissenters have put racial justice and reconciliation activities at the center of what needs to be done. There are reconciliation conferences, trips to Selma and Birmingham, Ala., study groups reading Martin Luther King Jr. and Howard Thurman. Evangelicals played important roles in the abolitionist movement; these Christians are trying to connect with that legacy." Brooks quotes reconciliation leader David Bailey on the connection between orthodoxy and reconciliation: "We remind people that peacemaking and healing are core to the Christian identity. There is no way to do spiritual formation unless you practice healing and reconciliation."[10]

Bailey's reference to spiritual formation is rooted in what the apostle Paul calls "conforming to the image of [God's] Son." This forming process is a progression: "Get to know Jesus well, because the more you know Him, the more you'll love Him, and the more you love Him, the more you'll want to follow Him, and the more you follow Him, the more you'll become like Him, and the more you become like Him, the more you become yourself."[11] When we are formed (or "conformed to the image of [God's] Son"), we are distinctly ourselves and also distinctly reflective of the heart of Jesus. This means justice will percolate in us as a driving passion, because it is "the foundation of God's throne." In His kingdom, pursuing justice is as basic as breathing, and the "Son" is the embodiment of that value. So, when healing and reconciliation are *not* reflected in the common practice of the church, we conform Jesus into the image of a lesser god.

> When we make ourselves conduits for generosity, equality, advocacy, and responsibility in the world, we are expressing God's character and walking in the way of Jesus.

Justice is rooted in God's character, and to treat it as something we *do* rather than someone we *are* is not reflective of God's image in us. When we make ourselves conduits for generosity, equality, advocacy, and responsibility in the world, we are expressing God's character and walking in the way of Jesus. People who experience us living this way are also experiencing the person of Jesus. And when people experience the unedited person of Jesus, they generally have two reactions (to use Dr. Peter Kreeft's categories)—they want to worship Him, or they want to kill Him.[12]

Letter from a Birmingham Jail

In 1963, on an April morning just before Easter, Martin Luther King Jr. led a protest parade through the streets of Birmingham, Alabama, in an attempt to leverage white city leaders to meet with black organizers and settle a host of racist grievances. Because the parade violated a court injunction, King was arrested and put in jail for ten days. While he was incarcerated, eight prominent white church leaders published a statement calling on King, and Birmingham's black citizens, to abide by "law and order and common sense," not demonstrations that "incite to hatred and violence" as the path to justice.

In response, King wrote a seven-thousand-word manifesto that is commonly called "Letter from a Birmingham Jail." In it, King offers a gracious but searing rebuttal to the religious critiques of his white clergymen "brothers." It's a masterful, beautifully written defense of God's heart for justice, and the vigorous courage required to live it out in a culture that punishes and kills its prophets. It's written to church leaders, in much the same way the apostle Paul wrote "corrective" letters to his church-plants around the world.

The letter builds to a crescendo at the end, with MLK declaring that a church known for ignoring or explaining away issues of justice is on its way to becoming irrelevant:

> The contemporary church is a weak, ineffectual voice. . . . So often it is an archdefender of the status quo. Far from being disturbed by the presence of the church, the power structure of the average community is consoled by the church's silent—and often even vocal—sanction of things as they are. . . . If today's church does not recapture the sacrificial spirit of the early church, it will lose its authenticity, forfeit the loyalty of millions, and be dismissed as an irrelevant social club with no meaning for the twentieth century. Every day I meet young people whose disappointment with the church has turned into outright disgust.[13]

These excerpted lines from MLK's letter are just as relevant today as they were six decades ago. Young people today are leaving the church in droves, and their reasons for leaving would resonate with Dr. King. The church *does* feel like "an irrelevant social club" to them, full of hypocritical and judgmental people who are "archdefenders of the status quo." A massive survey of thirteen- to twenty-five-year-old Christians reveals profound disparities between issues they say are important to them and issues the church sees as important—most of them justice-related. Here's a sampler of the gaps between what young people care about and what they believe the church cares about:

- Racial Justice (a 21 percent gap)
- Immigration Rights (a 23 percent gap)
- Income Inequality (a 23 percent gap)
- Disability Rights (a 22 percent gap)

Almost all young people (81 percent) say that "Racial Justice" is important to them, making it their top concern on a list of ten issues they care about.[14] But we live with competing priorities, and (as IJM's Gary Haugen points out) many influencing the contemporary church have not prioritized issues of justice. A case in point: a top church consulting organization, one that works with many of the largest and fastest-growing churches in the US, lists the top ten priorities churches should be "grading":

1. Emphasize personal evangelism and prayer.
2. Teach and promote the power of an invitation.
3. Catalyze action and decisions through weekend worship and teaching.
4. View the weekend services as a total experience.
5. Monitor spiritual movement and growth at all levels.
6. Focus on connecting people as quickly as possible.
7. Build steps not programs.
8. Become known in the community.
9. Purposefully communicate.
10. Limit non-strategic ministries.[15]

Conspicuously absent, of course, is anything related to God's priority, first on the prophet Micah's list: "To do justice . . ." (Mic. 6:8 NASB). In our determination to build bigger and better churches, we have forgotten that Jesus wants to infect our hearts with His passion for the marginalized, abused, and denigrated. The list of "complaints" sourced from young people is prophetic, because they are spotlighting the desperate needs of the marginalized, which are central to the heart of God and the mission of Jesus.

But we can "kill" these prophets by diminishing their concerns as the entitled whining of a "woke" generation. When we do, we must treat Jesus' own complaints as entitled whining: "What sorrow awaits you Pharisees! For you are careful to tithe even the tiniest income from your herb gardens, but you ignore justice and the love of God. You should tithe, yes, but do not neglect the more important things" (Luke 11:42). Here Jesus overlaps justice with God's love—Jesus is saying they're the same thing. God's love is expressed through justice; God's justice is expressed through His love.

When we turn a blind eye to the injustice around us, we are declining to "love God with all our heart" and to "love our neighbor as ourselves." This is the core of King's message to the church—and he paid the ultimate price for it when he was assassinated on the balcony of his room at the Lorraine Motel in Memphis, on April 4, 1968.

The Heart of the Messiah

In Matthew's account of the life and ministry of Jesus, he describes the de-captivating way He enters into the lives of the poor and marginalized, recalling Isaiah's prophecy about the coming Messiah:

"Look at my Servant, whom I have chosen.
    He is my Beloved, who pleases me.
I will put my Spirit upon him,
    and he will proclaim justice to the nations.
He will not fight or shout
    or raise his voice in public.
He will not crush the weakest reed
    or put out a flickering candle.
    Finally he will cause justice to be victorious.
And his name will be the hope
    of all the world."
(Isa. 42:1–4; Matt. 12:15–21)

Because the Christian church is also the body of Christ in the world—the interconnected and organic extension of the Messiah—our name is supposed to be "the hope of all the world." When people consider what a Christian is and does, are we "proclaiming justice to the nations" and protecting "flickering candles"? Are we considered "the hope of the world"? When the world does not agree with these descriptions, it's time to step back and consider whether our reputation as unconscious "defenders of the status quo" is overshadowing our call to live out the mission of Jesus in the world.

When a "low-life" Canaanite woman begs Jesus to heal her demon-oppressed daughter (Matt. 15:21–28), Jesus shrewdly responds to her in a way guaranteed to spotlight the bigotry of the Jews surrounding Him: "It isn't right to take food from the children and throw it to the dogs." When she responds to this common degradation with courageous and trusting abandon, Jesus delights in her. He's turning the tables on the injustice she's suffered by loudly proclaiming her courage to the crowds, who are shocked by His advocacy: "Dear woman, your faith is great. Your request is granted."

Let's return to the place we started—Gary Haugen's response to those who see justice as a distraction from the core message of the gospel: "It would be hard to look at the biblical text and think that justice was a distraction, since of course, it says that justice and righteousness are the foundation of God's throne."[16] If we embrace this observation, based on the overwhelming evidence of Jesus' own teaching and mission in the world, the centrality of justice as a theme in all of the Bible, and the justice-focused influence of theologians and thought leaders both historically (C. S. Lewis, Karl Barth, Henri Nouwen) and in the contemporary church (Sarah Coakley, N. T. Wright, Esau McCaulley), the outcome is not simply rhetorical. This truth changes the lens through which we see all of life. And when that happens, we open ourselves to the Spirit acting through us to seed justice in our everyday life because that's what distinguishes a disciple of Jesus.

Walking the Way of (the Unedited) Jesus

What will it look like if we walk in the way of the unedited Jesus, living our life with a heightened sensitivity to the injustice all around us, and motivated by love to make ourselves available in every way to advance the cause of justice in the world? Consider these two macro-filters:

1. We live the life of a disciple, embracing the way Jesus understands the rabbi/talmid relationship.

Our faith is formed in us not through self-discipline, but through relational *infection*. This is how the ancient rabbis of Jesus' time shaped their talmids, or apprentices—it was much more than a student/teacher relationship. Again, Jesus described it using His Vine/Branch illustration, reiterating the "mechanics" of a discipling relationship twice for emphasis: "Remain in me, and I will remain in you. For a branch cannot produce fruit if it is severed from the vine, and you cannot be fruitful unless you remain in me. Yes, I am the vine; you are the branches. Those who remain in me, and I in them, will produce much fruit. For apart from me you can do nothing" (John 15:4–5).

To be formed by Jesus is to remain in Him. For a talmid, that meant leaving your parents and your community to live in the same household with your Rabbi—eating together, learning together, laughing together, weeping together. The life of a talmid meant immersive togetherness. And that's the best way to describe what "remain" means. For us, the obvious follow-up question is: *How do we remain in someone we can't see, hear, touch, taste, or smell?*

There is no more important question for us to answer in our life—it is central to everything. Think of "remaining" as a direct expression of Jesus' branch-in-the-vine metaphor. It is union and communion at the most intimate level. In his fantasy novel *At the Back of the North Wind*, the great Scottish writer and pastor George MacDonald explores "remaining" in this interchange between the little boy Diamond and his mother. Diamond is singing a lullaby to his baby sister, whom he has nicknamed "Dulcimer." His mother has never heard the song before.

"You never made that song, Diamond," said his mother.

"No, mother. I wish I had. No, I don't. That would be to take it from somebody else. But it's mine for all that."

"What makes it yours?"

"I love it so."

"Does loving a thing make it yours?"

"I think so, mother—at least more than anything else can. If I didn't love baby (which couldn't be, you know) she wouldn't be mine a bit. But I do love baby, and baby is my very own Dulcimer."

"The baby's mine, Diamond."

"That makes her the more mine, mother."

"How do you make that out?"

"Because you're mine, mother."

"Is that because you love me?"

"Yes, just because. Love makes the only myness," said Diamond.[17]

When we come to love Jesus as He really is, not the edited versions of Him that strip away the beauty of His magnetic and confounding personality, we are entering into "myness" with Him. Remaining in Him means to behold this beauty—to savor the way He seeds justice in the world until His otherness saturates our soul, and we are infected with a deep love for Him. It means we slow down to comprehend His words and actions in the gospel accounts, and in the direct experiences of His followers who were released from captivity by Him. It means we continually pause to invite the Spirit to show us His heart for those experiencing injustice as we read or pray: "The Spirit of truth . . . will come to you from the Father and will testify all about me" (John 15:26). It means we focus on His emotional responses to injustice, drinking deeply from His indignation and fury. When we do, we soon find ourselves feeling what Jesus feels for the oppressed and needy, making ourselves a conduit for His justice in the world.

Henri Nouwen describes this discipling/remaining progression toward justice as our foundation: "God's compassion is the source of all human compassion, and . . . our compassion is therefore nothing more or less than a participation in and a reflection of this divine compassion. Discipleship in the Christian sense is the realization that without Christ compassion is indeed impossible, but that with, through, and in him it has no limits. . . . In Christ, we can carry the burden of the whole world. But his burden is a light burden."[18]

It's important to remember that, as we remain in the Vine, the Vine remains in us. Our discipleship is characterized by mutual pursuit, mutual delight, mutual knowing, and mutual respect. We do not have to *appropriate* Jesus' passion for justice, as if we are learning a new discipline or wielding a new tool. He will do the appropriating. We can bring the weight of our impact into daunting issues of injustice because it's His work through us, not our work through Him, that carries that weight. Our Rabbi's mission is to infect our hearts experientially, beyond intellectual assent, with the primacy of justice. To "taste and see" His goodness toward the victimized and marginalized means we ingest that goodness—it becomes a part of us.

---

2. We intercede and advocate, driven not by a great "supposed to," but by a great love.

Dr. King has already given us a blueprint for intercession and advocacy in his "Letter from a Birmingham Jail." From it, we recognize that injustice has underlying causes, and we are not afraid to explore them, or content to remain ignorant about them. This exploration necessarily happens in the context of relationship, and requires courage that is sourced in Jesus. Injustice is never undermined rhetorically, it is impacted through our brave relational investments. We know the "giants of advocacy"— MLK or Mother Teresa, for example—showed great courage in pursuing justice for "the least of these." But what hope do "average" people have for making a difference with what little they have to give? Well, the advance of justice in the world is *defined by* the micro-heroic acts of average people, lived out under the radar and away from the spotlight.

Before my wife, Bev, befriended a Syrian refugee family, arriving in our town after a harrowing escape from the death squads that terrorized their Damascus neighborhood, we had no personal connections to the refugee community. Five years later, Bev is embedded in it. The heart of Jesus in her is now relationally connected to a beloved people scarred by injustice—together, we *feel* their suffering and pain. And that means that the "immigration issue" is no longer a mere issue; it is contained in the faces of people we love. That morphs our view of fixing a broken immigration system from a political talking point to a kingdom-of-God necessity. We have borrowed the eyes of our friends so that we can better see what injustice looks like, and now we have what Jesus describes as "ears to hear and eyes to see" (see Matt. 13:16). Once our filter for understanding the world is changed, the way we interact with that world changes.

So, whose eyes are you borrowing? Your answer to that question could change your "average" life, the same way it has changed our average life.

Advocacy and intercession on behalf of those experiencing injustice is fueled by the conduit of our vertical relationship with Jesus and our horizontal warmth for them, backed by conviction.

The way we advance the cause of justice in the world happens in much the same way parents advance their children in the faith. In my work as Executive Director of Vibrant Faith, a ministry resourcing, training, coaching, and research organization founded by pioneering family ministry expert Dr. Merton Strommen, our team has been exploring the way parents intercede and advocate for faith maturity in their children. We know from decades of research that parents who have a "warm, authoritative" relationship with their kids, and an intimate, authentic relationship with Jesus tend to influence these children into a lifelong trajectory of faith.[19] Think of this as the nexus of a vertical line (intimacy with God) and a horizontal line (a warm but conviction-infused relationship with children). In that intersection, kids experience a transformational force we call *love*. It forms them. And in the same way, advocacy and intercession on behalf of those experiencing injustice is fueled by the conduit of our vertical relationship with Jesus and our horizontal warmth for them, backed by conviction. Once these two factors are in play, we are living in transformational spaces, where injustice is not only countered, but conquered.

To better envision this truth, here's a close-to-home story that reveals how "average" acts of advocacy can lead to epic outcomes.

My wife assists in an English as a Second Language (ESL) course for immigrants, asylum-seekers, and refugees. There, she met Hashem (not his real name), who had only recently arrived in America after a dangerous five-month journey to escape from his home country, which is led by a despotic regime. Hashem is a lawyer who served on a human rights commission at home. After traveling to an international conference on human rights, Hashem was followed, harassed, and eventually arrested in the middle of the night by authorities who (wrongly) suspected him of plotting to overthrow the government. He was thrown in prison, tortured, and released only after he agreed to give up his home as "bail." Once out, his parents urged him to flee the country, so he escaped with only what he could carry on his back. Abandoned by human smugglers and twice jailed, Hashem traveled (often on foot) through eleven countries, eventually landing in our town after strangers agreed to sponsor him. Those "rescuers" soon became yet another source of torment, threatening Hashem and demanding thousands of dollars from him.

As Bev connected with this traumatized man over several weeks, uncovering his story, she felt compelled to get involved in his plight so that others could help. She contacted refugee services, scouted for families who might be able to offer him safe lodging, and found a legal practice that could take his case. The beating heart of Jesus in her intersected with the warmth and conviction she developed when she learned Hashem's story. He now has a safe place to live, provision for his necessities, and is working with lawyers on an expedited path to asylum in the US.

This is how God's heart for justice in the world advances—one story at a time, leveraged by one average person's determined efforts, fueled by love.

Reflection/Discussion Questions for Individuals or Small Groups

The De-prioritizing
of Justice

- Why do you think so many who call themselves Christians have "forgotten" the priority of advocating for justice?

- In your own experience, what is the difference between fairness and justice?

- What is our responsibility to account for the injustices people experience in our nation?

- What's something that stuck out to you—or impacted you—from the excerpt of the Rev. Dr. Martin Luther King's "Letter From a Birmingham Jail"?

- Why is justice not higher on the list of priorities for most churches?

- As you have grown in your relationship with Jesus, how have you experienced yourself living out His priorities in your life?

- What are the biggest blocks to investing yourself in advocating for justice in your spheres of influence? In what ways have you felt nudged to make a difference?

EPILOGUE:

The De-fanging of Jesus

* * *

"I came not to bring peace, but a sword."
MATTHEW 10:34

The mission of Jesus begins in a world immersed in paganism, seasoned by Judaism. Paganism is polytheistic—adherents worship a diversity of gods, many embedded in nature, some demanding appeasement and, at its extreme, human sacrifice. It's syncretic, meaning pagan practice is spiritually fluid and accommodating of many religious expressions—like a roulette wheel of spiritual beliefs. In the time of Jesus, Judaism is seen as an outlier religious community defined by an exclusive claim that Israel alone represents God's chosen people. They are a mustard seed of monotheism planted in a vast garden of pagan and Hellenistic spirituality.

In the wake of the resurrection, the remaining disciples—eleven men and a contingent of women—get busy planting the church. They are mostly uneducated laborers, fishermen, or cultural pariahs from a backwater region in the vast Roman Empire.

The mission Jesus hands to these misfits is clearly broader than ancient Judaism's protective, insular defaults. First, He tells them to "go and make disciples of all the nations" (Matt. 28:19). We know this line from the Great Commission so well that the magnitude of the word "all" escapes us. The mission Jesus is giving His followers reaches way beyond their cultural and religious borders, obliterating any assumptions they have about who this "good news" is for.

Later, he gives Peter (the leader of the early church) a vision of "unclean" animals piled onto a sheet descending from heaven that he's to "kill and eat" (Acts 10). When Peter protests, Jesus corrects: "Do not call something unclean if God has made it clean." Then the Spirit of Jesus tells Peter that three Gentile ("unclean") men have come to see him, and that he should welcome them into his home and serve their needs. Peter obeys ("God has shown me that I should no longer think of anyone as impure or unclean"), and soon the mission of Jesus spreads with viral momentum. Now everyone, everywhere can join the "chosen ones" as brothers and sisters. Monotheism washes over the polytheistic world like a tidal wave, carrying away its smorgasbord spirituality. Three centuries later the Christian church numbers three million.

And now, two millennia later, we are in a full-circle moment—the decline of the church in the West means the primacy of a discipling relationship with Jesus is giving way to widespread pagan, syncretic norms. We are looking for new ways to be moral, to live as "good people" apart from a relationship with God, moving from a monogamous union with God to an open marriage. We have told ourselves we still believe in Jesus while our functional belief system is more pagan than Christian. *New York Times* columnist Ross Douthat says: "America [is] a nation of Christian heretics, if you will, in which traditional churches have been supplanted by self-help gurus and spiritual-political entrepreneurs. These figures cobble together pieces of the old orthodoxies, take out the inconvenient bits and pitch them to mass audiences that want part of the old-time religion but nothing too unsettling or challenging or ascetic."[1]

To account for this tension between how we self-identify and what we actually practice in our faith, our only recourse is to edit the real Jesus to fit the requirements of what is essentially a Christian façade hiding a neo-pagan belief system. He is a square peg that needs to fit into our round hole, so we whittle away at Him. But Jesus will not be diminished.

He has come with a sword, not peace, because He intends to remake us. He will do this at our invitation, and because of His deeper-than-deep love for us. And when we submit to the edge of His sword, we discover our re-formed identity is the deepest, truest version of ourselves. We find the deeply satisfying, beautiful "abundant life" He intended for us all along. Eugene Peterson was spot-on: "Every omitted detail of Jesus, so carefully conveyed to us by the Gospel writers, reduces Jesus. We need the whole Jesus. The complete Jesus. Everything he said. Every detail of what he did."[2]

Acknowledgments

Toward the end of an hour-long Q&A with Youth For Christ President Jake Bland, at an online gathering of the parachurch organization's US leadership, Jake asked me to pinpoint the top challenge facing the church today. I paused to chew on that for a moment, then I told those hundreds of YFC leaders there is no challenge more deeply rooted in the church than our propensity to edit Jesus. I didn't know it at the time, but that moment was the catalytic seed for this book. Thank you, Jake, for asking me the right question at the right time . . .

As both of my daughters are moving into adulthood, I'm experiencing the blessing of their maturity—their insights, convictions, and corrections are often prophetic in my life. And that's the case here. My younger daughter, Emma, signed on to help me get the word out about this book through various social media channels, using her considerable skills as a digital communicator. And I asked my older daughter, Lucy, on her way to medical school, to read this book as I was writing it. She's a gifted writer herself, and she invested what little margin she had into a deep dive—she's given me priceless feedback that has profoundly impacted the final version. Thank you, dears . . .

In that same spirit . . .

- I'm grateful to Bev, my wife, for your ongoing dialogue, passion for, and incisive input into this book, and your bulldog commitment to clarity.
- Thank you Dr. Dave Rahn, for the deep impact of your friendship in my life, and for your open-armed embracing of this book's mission—your feedback, creative suggestions, and filtering have infected this book with truth.
- Thanks to my team at Vibrant Faith for the way you stretch me, challenge me, and encourage me—I'm so grateful for you.
- Thanks to my agent, Greg Johnson, for your passionate and propelling response to the original book proposal, and for your (always) incisive feedback.
- Thanks to our "home church" of two-dozen young people, who have been co-discoverers with me as we plumb the depths of Jesus' heart. Our kindred pursuit of "the heart of Jesus, not His recipes" has threaded prophetic truth into these pages. Translation: I've stolen your best discoveries.
- And thanks to Drew Dyck at Moody, for seizing on the possibilities in this work and for stepping up to champion it, and Connor Sterchi for your careful, thoughtful input and shaping of the final manuscript.

Finally, I'm so deeply grateful to you, Jesus, for inviting me (again) to adventure with You in this work over the last three years. The knife-edge of trust required to create together is fuel for my intimacy with You—You are the real prize, no matter what happens with the work we do together.

Notes

Introduction

1. Referencing language in Matthew 7:13–14.
2. Eugene Peterson, from the foreword in Mark Galli, *Jesus Mean and Wild: The Unexpected Love of an Untamable God* (Grand Rapids, MI: Baker Books), 11.
3. Gregory A. Smith, "About Three-in-Ten US Adults Are Now Religiously Unaffiliated," Pew Research Center, December 14, 2021, https://www.pewresearch.org/religion/2021/12/14/about-three-in-ten-u-s-adults-are-now-religiously-unaffiliated/.
4. Ibid.
5. Christian Smith and Melissa Lundquist Denton, *Soul Searching: The Religious and Spiritual Lives of American Teenagers* (Oxford: Oxford University Press, 2009), 165.
6. Russell Moore, "Integrity and the Future of the Church," *Plough*, October 5, 2021, https://www.plough.com/en/topics/faith/witness/integrity-and-the-future-of-the-church.
7. Scot McKnight, "Bored Out of Our Faith," in Jesus Creed, *Christianity Today* Blog Forum, August 26, 2022, https://www.christianitytoday.com/scot-mcknight/2022/august/bored-out-of-our-faith.html.
8. Derek Thompson, "Three Decades Ago, America Lost Its Religion—Why?," *The Atlantic*, September 26, 2019.
9. Nicole Winfield, "A Pope, Scholar Dies at Age 95," *Denver Post*, January 1, 2023.

10. Sarah C. P. Williams, "Selfish Sheep Seek the Center," Science.org, July 23, 2012, https://www.science.org/content/article/selfish-sheep-seek-center.

11. Christian Wiman, *My Bright Abyss: Meditation of a Modern Believer* (New York: Farrar, Straus and Giroux, 2014), 11, 49–50.

12. From the nationwide "GROUP Magazine Survey of Workcamp Participants," conducted by the author during the summer of 2008.

13. Sumit Paul-Choudhury, "Tomorrow's Gods: What Is the Future of Religion," BBC, August 1, 2019, https://www.bbc.com/future/article/20190801-tomorrows-gods-what-is-the-future-of-religion.

14. "American Worldview Inventory 2020 – At a Glance: AWVI 2020 Results – Release #8: Perceptions of Sin and Salvation," Cultural Research Center, Arizona Christian University, August 4, 2020, https://www.arizonachristian.edu/wp-content/uploads/2020/08/AWVI-2020-Release-08-Perceptions-of-Sin-and-Salvation.pdf.

15. "Most American Christians Do Not Believe That Satan or the Holy Spirit Exist," Barna Group, April 13, 2009, https://www.barna.com/research/most-american-christians-do-not-believe-that-satan-or-the-holy-spirit-exist/.

16. N. T. Wright, *Following Jesus* (Grand Rapids, MI: Eerdmans, 2014), xiv.

Chapter 1: The Comingling of Kingdoms

1. "The Alliance Between Church and Empire," Britannica, https://www.britannica.com/topic/Christianity/The-alliance-between-church-and-empire.

2. Wendy Doniger, ed., "Constantine I," in *Britannica Encyclopedia of World Religions* (Encyclopædia Britannica, 2006), 262.

3. Marc Cortez, "What Does Heresy Mean?," Christianity.com, February 7, 2024, https://www.christianity.com/wiki/christian-terms/what-does-heresy-mean.html.

4. Eric E. Peterson and Eugene H. Peterson, *Letters to a Young Pastor: Timothy Conversations Between Father and Son* (Colorado Springs: NavPress, 2020), 98–99.

5. "Who Killed Mars Hill?," *The Rise & Fall of Mars Hill* podcast, episode 1.

6. Tara Ross, "This Day In History: The First Continental Congress Opens in Prayer," September 5, 2020.

7. David L. Holmes, *The Faiths of the Founding Fathers*, illustrated ed. (Oxford: Oxford University Press, 2006), 134.

8. "Religion and the Founding of the American Republic: Religion and the Congress of the Confederation, 1774–89," Library of Congress, https://www.loc.gov/exhibits/religion/rel04.html.

9. Ibid.

10. Holmes, *Founding Fathers*, 225.

11. Jerry Robinson, "Do You Agree with America's Founders About Jesus Christ?," YouTube, May 21, 2020, https://www.youtube.com/watch?v=yEP39YSF2Vk.

12. Shamir Brice, "A Classy Constitution: Classical Influences on the United States Constitution from Ancient Greek and Roman History and Political Thought," John Carroll University, 2015.

13. From a sermon preached by Dr. Timothy Keller at Redeemer Presbyterian Church on January 31, 2010.

14. Gregory A. Smith, Michael Rotolo, and Patricia Tevington, "3. Views of the U.S. as a 'Christian Nation' and Opinions About 'Christian Nationalism,'" Pew Research Center, October 27, 2022, https://www.pewresearch.org/religion/2022/10/27/views-of-the-u-s-as-a-christian-nation-and-opinions-about-christian-nationalism/.

15. Timothy Dalrymple, "Why Evangelicals Disagree on the President," *Christianity Today*, November 2, 2020, https://www.christianitytoday.com/ct/2020/november-web-only/trump-election-politics-church-kingdom.html.

16. "American Piety in the 21st Century: Insights to the Depth and Complexity of Religion in the US," Baylor Institute for Studies of Religion, September 2006, https://www.baylor.edu/content/services/document.php/33304.pdf.

17. "A Christian Nation?: Understanding the Threat of Christian Nationalism to American Democracy and Culture," Public Religion Research Institute and the Brookings Institution, February 8, 2023, https://www.prri.org/wp-content/uploads/2023/02/PRRI-Jan-2023-Christian-Nationalism-Final.pdf.

18. John Blake, "The Relentless Focus on White Christian Nationalism Is Spreading a Racist Myth," CNN, February 3, 2024, https://www.cnn.com/2024/02/03/us/white-christian-nationalism-racist-myth-cec/index.html.

19. From the podcast *This Cultural Moment*, season 1, episode 1, cohosted by Mark Sayers and John Mark Comer, 3:10–3:25.

20. "The Aftermath," *The Rise and Fall of Mars Hill* podcast, episode 12, December 4, 2021.

21. John Blake, "The Evangelical Church Faces a 'State of Emergency' over the Pandemic and Politics, Andy Stanley Says," CNN, Saturday, June 4, 2022, https://www.cnn.com/2022/06/04/us/andy-stanley-evangelicals-book-blake-cec/index.html.

22. Quoted in David Brooks, "The Dissenters Trying to Save Evangelicalism from Itself," *New York Times*, February 4, 2022, https://www.nytimes.com/2022/02/04/opinion/evangelicalism-division-renewal.html.

23. From Zack Stanton, "You Need to Take the Religious Left Seriously This Time," *Politico*, February 25, 2021, https://www.politico.com/news/magazine/2021/02/25/religious-left-politics-liberal-471640.

24. From the "Moore to the Point" newsletter published by *Christianity Today*, January 19, 2023, https://christianitytoday.activehosted.com/index.php?action=social&chash=454cecc4829279e64d624cd8a8c9ddf1.12055&s=cb7cdbfdc5fcf9cd369b72bd761107e4.

25. "Americans Say Serving the Needy Is Christianity's Biggest Contribution to Society," Barna Research, October 25, 2010, https://www.barna.com/research/americans-say-serving-the-needy-is-christianitys-biggest-contribution-to-society/.

26. David French, "Getting 'More Christians into Politics' Is the Wrong Christian Goal," *The Dispatch*, March 27, 2022, https://thedispatch.com/newsletter/frenchpress/getting-more-christians-into-politics/.

27. John Ortberg, *Who Is This Man?* (Grand Rapids, MI: Zondervan, 2012), 11–12.

28. "Learning from the Iranian Church—Brittany White and David Yeghnazar," from the *More than Me* podcast produced by Red Church in Melbourne, Australia, September 25, 2022.

29. French, "Getting 'More Christians into Politics' Is the Wrong Christian Goal."

30. From the Global Slavery Index at walkfree.org.

31. From "Why Was Slavery Abolished: Three Theories," by Trevor Getz, Professor of African and World History at San Francisco State University, Kahn Academy, kahnacademy.org.

32. Timothy Keller, "How Do Christians Fit into the Two-Party System? They Don't," *New York Times*, September 29, 2018, https://www.nytimes.com/2018/09/29/opinion/sunday/christians-politics-belief.html.

33. Tracy Kidder, *Mountains Beyond Mountain* (New York: Random House, 2009), 215.

34. Thane M. Erickson et al., "Compassionate and Self-Image Goals as Interpersonal Maintenance Factors in Clinical Depression and Anxiety," *Journal of Clinical Psychology*, September 12, 2017.

35. Therese Borchard, "Want to Lessen Your Depression? Help Someone" Everyday Health, March 6, 2015, everydayhealth.com.

36. Derek Thompson, "How America Lost Its Religion," *The Atlantic*, September 26, 2019, https://www.theatlantic.com/ideas/archive/2019/09/atheism-fastest-growing-religion-us/598843/.

37. Gregory Porter, "Take Me to the Alley," *Take Me to the Alley* (Blue Note, March 4, 2016). Used with permission.

Chapter 2: The Softening of Hard

1. Christian Smith and Amy Adamczyk, *Handing Down the Faith: How Parents Pass Their Religion On to the Next Generation* (Oxford: Oxford University Press, 2021), 41.

2. Ibid., 62.

3. Bob Smietana, "Americans Believe in Heaven, Hell, and a Little Bit of Heresy," Lifeway Research, October 28, 2014, https://research.lifeway.com/2014/10/28/americans-believe-in-heaven-hell-and-a-little-bit-of-heresy/.

4. "What Do Americans Believe About Jesus? 5 Popular Beliefs," Barna Group, April 1, 2015, https://www.barna.com/research/what-do-americans-believe-about-jesus-5-popular-beliefs/.

5. David Foster Wallace, *Infinite Jest* (New York: Back Bay Books, 2006), 973.

6. David Brooks, "Five Lies Our Culture Tells," *New York Times*, April 15, 2019, https://www.nytimes.com/2019/04/15/opinion/cultural-revolution-meritocracy.html.

7. Peter Kreeft, "The Shocking Life of Jesus" Saddleback Church's Ahmanson Lecture series, December 18, 2010.

8. Ruth Terry, "The Christian Right and Left Share the Same Faith But Couldn't Be More Different," *Yes!*, December 24, 2019, https://www.yesmagazine.org/social-justice/2019/12/24/political-christian-belief.

9. From a Pew Research Study of 6,500 American adults, conducted between September 20 and 26, 2021.

10. Leslie Schmucker, "The Uncomfortable Subject Jesus Addressed More than Anyone Else," The Gospel Coalition, May 11, 2017, https://www.thegospelcoalition.org/article/the-uncomfortable-subject-jesus-addressed-more-than-anyone-else/.

11. Smietana, "Americans Believe in Heaven, Hell, and a Little Bit of Heresy."

12. Christian Smith with Patricia Snell, *Souls in Transition: The Religious and Spiritual Lives of Emerging Adults* (Oxford: Oxford University Press, 2009), 167.

13. "US Religious Knowledge Survey: An Overview of the Pew Forum Survey, Results and Implications," Pew Research Center, September 28, 2010, https://www.pewresearch.org/religion/2010/09/28/us-religious-knowledge-an-overview-of-the-pew-forum-survey-results-and-implications/.

14. From *The Good Place*, season 1, episode 1.

15. Zack Stanton, "You Need to Take the Religious Left Seriously This Time," *Politico*, February 25, 2021, https://www.politico.com/news/magazine/2021/02/25/religious-left-politics-liberal-471640.

16. From Drew Dyck's Twitter post on September 13, 2018.

17. From a short talk by Dr. Conrad Gempf at the Simply Jesus gathering, July of 2018.

Chapter 3: The Marginalization of the Poor

1. From the Emperor Julian's "Letter to Arsacius," quoted in "Julian the Apostate's Lesson on Why We Are Good," by Steve Weidenkopf, published in Catholic Answers, November 9, 2016.

2. "Church Giving Stats and Strategies for Adapting to New Trends," Vanco, https://www.vancopayments.com/egiving/asset-church-giving-statistics-tithing.

3. John Lee, "Who Are the Most Generous? Not Who You'd Expect," *Christianity Today*, August 13, 2020, https://www.christianitytoday.com/ct/2020/august-web-only/most-generous-not-who-you-expect-vertical-generosity.html.

4. Electa Draper, "1 in 4 Americans Can't Think of Recent Positive Contribution by Christians," *Denver Post*, October 25, 2010, https://www.denverpost.com/2010/10/25/1-in-4-americans-cant-think-of-recent-positive-contribution-by-christians/.

5. "5 Reasons Millennials Stay Connected to Church," Barna Group, September 17, 2013, https://www.barna.com/research/5-reasons-millennials-stay-connected-to-church/; "5 Ways to Connect with Millennials," Barna Group, September 9, 2014, https://www.barna.com/research/5-ways-to-connect-with-millennials/.

6. Andrew Wilson, "Why Jesus, Not Salvation, Is God's Greatest Gift to Us," *Christianity Today*, August 22, 2016, https://www.christianitytoday.com/ct/2016/september/why-jesus-not-salvation-is-gods-greatest-gift-to-us.html.

7. Larry Lasiter, "A World Without Jesus?," Points of Truth Ministries, 2000.

8. From Bono's (Paul Hewson's) remarks at the National Prayer Breakfast in Washington, DC, February 2, 2006.

9. Rick Lawrence, *Jesus-Centered Daily: See. Hear. Touch. Smell. Taste* (Group Publishing, 2020), February 17.

10. Benoit Denizet-Lewis, "Why Are More American Teenagers than Ever Suffering from Severe Anxiety?," *New York Times*, October 17, 2017, https://www.nytimes.com/2017/10/11/magazine/why-are-more-american-teenagers-than-ever-suffering-from-severe-anxiety.html.

11. David Brooks, "Five Lies Our Culture Tells," *New York Times*, April 15, 2019, https://www.nytimes.com/2019/04/15/opinion/cultural-revolution-meritocracy.html.

12. Robby Gallaty, *The Forgotten Jesus: How Western Christians Should Follow an Eastern Rabbi* (Grand Rapids, MI: Zondervan, 2017), 96–97.

13. From an interview with Adam Young, conducted by my Vibrant Faith team on June 15, 2022.

14. "US Media Consumption (2021–2025)," Oberlo, https://www.oberlo.com/statistics/us-media-consumption.

15. Nicholas Kristof, "He's Jesus Christ," *New York Times*, June 27, 2015, https://www.nytimes.com/2015/06/28/opinion/sunday/nicholas-kristof-hes-jesus-christ.html.

Chapter 4: The Problem with Principles

1. From a talk by Dr. Dallas Willard at The Downing House in Denver, Colorado, January 3, 2010.

2. From "75 Most Popular Sermon Topics Being Preached Today," published on the Sermon Search website, January 4, 2022.

3. Ibid.

4. From Ray Ortlund's post on Twitter, April 27, 2022.

5. Taken from the YouTube video "Grafting Fruit Trees," produced by Daley's Fruit Tree Nursery in Kyogle, Australia.

6. Ibid.

7. John Kay, *Obliquity* (New York: Penguin Group, 2010), 71.

8. Peter Kreeft, *You Can Understand the Bible* (Ignatius Press: 2009), xii.

9. "The Aftermath," *The Rise and Fall of Mars Hill* podcast, episode 12.

10. Christian Smith and Melinda Lundquist Denton, *Soul Searching: The Religious and Spiritual Lives of American Teenagers* (Oxford: Oxford University Press, 2005), 164.

11. CRC Staff, "Counterfeit Christianity: 'Moralistic Therapeutic Deism' Most Popular Worldview in US Culture," Cultural Research Center at Arizona Christian University, April 27, 2021, https://www.arizonachristian.edu/2021/04/27/counterfeit-christianity-moralistic-therapeutic-deism-most-popular-worldview-in-u-s-culture/.

12. Ibid.

13. "Self-Help Books Statistics," Words Rated, December 2022, https://wordsrated.com/self-help-books-statistics/

14. "In U.S., Decline of Christianity Continues at Rapid Pace," Pew Research Center, October 17, 2019, https://www.pewresearch.org/religion/2019/10/17/in-u-s-decline-of-christianity-continues-at-rapid-pace/.

15. From "Self-Help Book Sales Are Rising Fast in the US, the NPD Group Says," January 12, 2019.

16. Garrison Keillor, *The Lake Wobegon Virus*, Audio Book Chapter 21—18:10 to 18:51, Arcade (September 29, 2020).

17. Ken Curtis, "The Spread of the Early Church," Christianity.com, updated August 18, 2023), https://www.christianity.com/church/church-history/the-spread-of-the-early-church-11629561.html.

18. Christian Smith et al., "Religious Trajectories from the Teenage Years into the Emerging Adult Years," *Lifelong Faith* (Summer 2010).

19. Ibid.

20. George MacDonald, *Discovering the Character of God* (Bloomington, MN: Bethany House, 1989), 199–200.

21. From Martin Luther King's Nobel Peace Prize acceptance speech, December 11, 1964.

22. Mark Sayers, *A Non-Anxious Presence* (Chicago: Moody Publishers, 2022), 133–134.

23. Ibid., 135.

24. "2022 State of American Theology," Lifeway Research and Ligonier Ministries, September 2022.

25. David French, "How Hypocrisy Drives Unbelief," *The Dispatch*, October 16, 2022, https://www.cnn.com/2022/06/04/us/andy-stanley-evangelicals-book-blake-cec/index.html.

26. "The Definition of Evil," Mathetis.org, https://www.mathetis.org/topic/the-definition-of-evil-wdgae/.

27. From an interview I conducted with author and founder of Wild at Heart Ministries John Eldredge, on July 3, 2018.

28. From the Trinity Forum's "Online Conversation: Jazz, Hope and the Gospel with William Edgar and Carl Ellis," August 5, 2022.

29. From an interview I conducted with author and founder of Wild at Heart Ministries John Eldredge, on July 3, 2018.

30. From a transcription of the 2005 Kenyon College Commencement Address, delivered by David Foster Wallace, May 21, 2005.

Chapter 5: The Golden-Calfing of Materialism

1. Randy Alcorn, "Ten Ways Materialism Brings Us to Ruin," ThinkEternity, January 24, 2023, https://thinke.org/blog/ten-ways-materialism-brings-us-to-ruin-randy-alcorn.

2. Jeffrey M. Jones, "US Church Membership Falls Below Majority for First Time," Gallup.com, March 21, 2021, https://news.gallup.com/poll/341963/church-membership-falls-below-majority-first-time.aspx.

3. "Competing Worldviews Influence Today's Christians," Barna Research, May 9, 2017, https://www.barna.com/research/competing-worldviews-influence-todays-christians/.

4. Marissa Postell Sullivan, "Prosperity Gospel Beliefs on the Rise among Churchgoers," Lifeway Research, August 22, 2023, https://research.lifeway.com/2023/08/22/prosperity-gospel-beliefs-on-the-rise-among-churchgoers/.

5. Rick Lawrence, "The Other American Dream," Vibrant Faith, January 16, 2023, https://vibrantfaith.org/american-dream/.

6. Samir S. Gupte, "The Reciprocal Reshaping of the American Dream and American Religion," Rollins College, August 2011, https://scholarship.rollins.edu/cgi/viewcontent.cgi?article=1014&context=mls.

7. Robert Wuthnow, "Pious Materialism: How Americans View Faith and Money," *The Christian Century* (March 3, 1993): 239–42.

8. Chris Lemann, *The Money Cult: Capitalism, Christianity, and the Unmaking of the American Dream* (New York: Melville House, 2017), 3.

9. Jonathan Haidt, "Why the Past 10 Years of American Life Have Been Uniquely Stupid," *The Atlantic*, April 11, 2022, https://www.theatlantic.com/magazine/archive/2022/05/social-media-democracy-trust-babel/629369/.

10. Wuthnow, "Pious Materialism," 239–42.

11. Jeroen Vaes and Steve Loughnan, eds., "Social Comparison, Personal Relative Deprivation, and Materialism," *British Journal of Social Psychology* 56, no. 2 (June 2017): 373–92.

12. H. Zhang et al., "Personal Relative Deprivation Boosts Materialism," *Basic and Applied Social Psychology* 37 (2015): 247–59.

13. "Educational Attainment," National Center for Education Statistics, Institute of Education Sciences, retrieved January 16, 2020.

14. Roy Y. Chan, "Understanding the Purpose of Higher Education: An Analysis of the Economic and Social Benefits for Completing a College Degree," *Journal of Education Policy, Planning and Administration* 6, no. 5 (2006): 2.
15. "Re-Monking the Church," *Christianity Today*, September 2, 2005.
16. Steve Farrar, *Family Survival in the American Jungle* (Colorado Springs: Multnomah Press, 1991), 63.
17. From an interview I conducted with author and founder of Wild at Heart Ministries, John Eldredge, on July 3, 2018.
18. Robert Hanrott, "Epicureanism After Epicurus—The Influence of Epicurus on Western Thought," Epicurus Today, https://epicurus.today/epicureanism-after-epicurus-the-influence-of-epicurus-on-western-thought/.
19. "Competing Worldviews Influence Today's Christians," Barna Research, May 9, 2017, https://www.barna.com/research/competing-worldviews-influence-todays-christians/.
20. Wendell Berry, "A Native Hill," *The Hudson Review* 21, no. 4 (Winter 1968–1969): 601–34.
21. Kyle Roberts, "When Churches Conflate Christianity and Nationalism (10 Consequences)," Progressive Christian, June 28, 2017.
22. "Faith and the American Dream," The American Enterprise Institute's Initiative on Faith & Public Life, January 13, 2011, https://faithandpubliclife.com/faith-and-the-american-dream/.
23. From a transcription of the film *Jerry and Marge Go Large*, screenplay written by Jason Fagone and Brad Copeland, released June 17, 2022.
24. C. S. Lewis, *Mere Christianity* (New York: Harper Collins, 2001), 226–27.

Chapter 6: The Dismissing of the Supernatural

1. Bart D. Ehrman, "Inside the Conversion Tactics of the Early Christian Church," History.com, March 29, 2018, https://www.history.com/news/inside-the-conversion-tactics-of-the-early-christian-church.
2. C. S. Lewis, *Miracles*, rev. ed. (New York: HarperOne, 2015), 5–6.
3. Gregory A. Boyd and Paul Rhodes Eddy, *Lord or Legend: Wrestling with the Jesus Dilemma* (Grand Rapids, MI: Baker Books, 2007), 22.
4. Scott Bessenecker, "Through My Lens—American Christian Syncretism," InterVarsity.org, January 30, 2020, https://intervarsity.org/blog/through-my-lens-american-christian-syncretism.
5. C. S. Lewis, *God in the Dock: Essays on Theology and Ethics* (Grand Rapids, MI: Eerdmans, 1970), 81.
6. "Many Americans Mix Multiple Faiths," Pew Research Center, December 9, 2009, https://www.pewresearch.org/religion/2009/12/09/many-americans-mix-multiple-faiths/.
7. "The Religious Typology," Pew Research Center, August 29, 2018, https://www.pewresearch.org/religion/2018/08/29/the-religious-typology/.

8. "New Poll Finds Even Religious Americans Feel the Good Vibrations," Religion News Service, August 29, 2018, https://religionnews.com/2018/08/29/new-poll-finds-even-religious-americans-feel-the-good-vibrations/.

9. Ibid.

10. Jon Stewart, *An Introduction to Hegel's Lectures on the Philosophy of Religion: The Issue of Religious Content in the Enlightenment and Romanticism* (Oxford: Oxford University Press, 2022), 26–27.

11. "Quotes From John Wimber," vineyardusa.org.

Chapter 7: The Siren Song of Platforming

1. Jeff Goins, "Why Building Your Own Platform Is Essential," goinswriter.com, https://goinswriter.com/platform/.

2. Tom Peters, "The Brand Called You," Fast Company, August 31, 1997, https://www.fastcompany.com/28905/brand-called-you.

3. Emma Goldberg, "Burned Out On Your Personal Brand," *New York Times*, October 20, 2022 https://www.nytimes.com/2022/10/20/business/influencer-burn-out-jobs.html.

4. Jonathan Haidt, "Why the Past 10 Years of American Life Have Been Uniquely Stupid," *The Atlantic*, April 11, 2022, https://www.theatlantic.com/magazine/archive/2022/05/social-media-democracy-trust-babel/629369/.

5. Stacy Jo Dixon, "Number of Global Social Network Users 2017–2027," Statista, August 29, 2023, https://www.statista.com/statistics/278414/number-of-worldwide-social-network-users/.

6. Sarah Green Carmichael, "The Perils of Self-Promotion," *Harvard Business Review*, January–February 2014, https://hbr.org/2014/01/the-perils-of-self-promotion.

7. David Leonhart, "The Phone in the Room," *New York Times*, February 27, 2023, https://www.nytimes.com/2023/02/27/briefing/phones-mental-health.html.

8. "Bonus: Asbury University Outpouring with Pete Greig," *Rebuilders Podcast*, February 21, 2023, https://www.youtube.com/watch?v=pHpfpencbtI.

9. Jamie Morgan, "10 Tips to Build a Godly Platform," Charisma News, September 20, 2018, https://cn.mycharisma.com/marketplace/10-tips-to-build-a-godly-platform/.

10. "Everything Is Still Falling Apart," *The Rise & Fall of Mars Hill* podcast, episode 15.

11. Henri Nouwen, *In the Name of Jesus: Reflections on Christian Leadership* (Chestnut Ridge, PA: Crossroad Publishing Company, 1992), 28–30.

12. Katelyn Beaty, *Celebrities for Jesus* (Grand Rapids, MI: Brazos Press, 2022), 8.

13. Mark Travers, "3 Key Indicators of a Life Well-Lived," *Psychology Today*, March 9, 2022, https://www.psychologytoday.com/us/blog/social-instincts/202203/3-key-indicators-of-a-life-well-lived.

14. C. S. Lewis, *The Weight of Glory and Other Addresses* (New York: Macmillan Publishing Group, 1980), 18–19.

15. "Practicing Gratitude: An Online Conversation with Diana Butler Bass," Trinity Forum, November 19, 2021.

16. "I'll Take the Encouragement, but I'll Pass the Glory On," 21CenturyPilgrim .home.com, September 30, 2019, https://21centurypilgrim.home.blog/2019/ 09/30/ill-take-the-encouragement-but-ill-pass-the-glory-on/.

17. Rick Warren, *The Purpose-Driven Life* (Grand Rapids, MI: Zondervan, 2013), 149.

18. Mark Sayers, "The Difference Between 'Platform' and Pastoral Leadership," interview by Drew Dyck, *Christianity Today*, November 10, 2014, https://www .christianitytoday.com/ct/2014/october/platform-and-pastoral-leadership-mark-sayers.html.

19. J. N. Figgis and R. V. Laurence, eds., "Letter to Bishop Mandell Creighton, April 5, 1887," in *Historical Essays and Studies* (London: Macmillan, 1907).

Chapter 8: The De-prioritizing of Justice

1. "Doing Justice," Trinity Forum interview with Gary Haugen, February 4, 2022.

2. Ibid.

3. Daniel A. Cox, "Generation Z and the Future of Faith in America," American Enterprise Institute, March 24, 2022.

4. Karl Zinmeister, "Less God, Less Giving?," *Philanthropy Magazine* (Winter 2019), https://www.philanthropyroundtable.org/magazine/less-god-less-giving/.

5. Ibid.

6. Ibid.

7. Ibid.

8. Ibid.

9. Timothy Keller, *The Reason for God* (New York: Penguin Books, 2009), 61.

10. David Brooks, "The Dissenters Trying to Save Evangelicalism from Itself," *New York Times*, February 2, 2022, https://www.nytimes.com/2022/02/04/opinion/ evangelicalism-division-renewal.html.

11. I first heard "The Progression" from my friend Ned Erickson, who is the founder and director of the Winston-Salem Fellows in North Carolina.

12. From Peter Kreeft's lecture "The Shocking Beauty of Jesus," given at Gordon-Conwell Seminary on September 20, 2007, and later expanded upon in his book *Jesus-Shock* (St. Augustine's Press, 2008).

13. From "Letter from a Birmingham Jail," by Martin Luther King Jr., April 16, 1963.

14. From "The State of Young People and Religion 2021," Springtide Research, October 25, 2021.

15. Bart Rendel, "10 Priorities of America's Top 100 Churches," Intentional Churches, September 30, 2016, https://intentionalchurches.com/10-priorities-weve-learned-americas-top-100-churches/.

16. "Doing Justice," Trinity Forum interview with Gary Haugen, February 4, 2022.

17. George MacDonald, *At the Back of the North Wind* (CreateSpace Independent Publishing Platform, 2017), 142.

18. From a speech by Henri J. M. Nouwen *on November 5, 1976*, at the Collegeville Institute in Collegeville, Minnesota.

19. This is the condensed result of many research findings over the years, but particularly the research of Dr. Christian Smith and his work with the National Study of Youth and Religion. The latest findings are in his book, *Handing Down the Faith: How Parents Pass Their Religion On to the Next Generation* (Oxford: Oxford University Press, 2021).

Epilogue: The De-fanging of Jesus

1. Ross Douthat, "The Return of Paganism," *New York Times*, December 12, 2018, https://www.nytimes.com/2018/12/12/opinion/christianity-paganism-america.html.

2. Eugene Peterson, from the foreword in Mark Galli, *Jesus Mean and Wild: The Unexpected Love of an Untamable God* (Grand Rapids, MI: Baker Books), 11.

You finished reading!

Did this book help you in some way? If so, please consider writing an honest review wherever you purchase your books. Your review gets this book into the hands of more readers and helps us continue to create biblically faithful resources.

Moody Publishers books help fund the training of students for ministry around the world.

The **Moody Bible Institute** is one of the most well-known Christian institutions in the world, training thousands of young people to faithfully serve Christ wherever He calls them. And when you buy and read a book from Moody Publishers, you're helping make that vital ministry training possible.

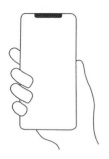

Continue to dive into the Word, *anytime, anywhere.*

Find what you need to take your next step in your walk with Christ: from uplifting music to sound preaching, our programs are designed to help you right when you need it.

Download the **Moody Radio App** and start listening today!

 MOODY
Publishers®

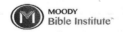 MOODY
Bible Institute™

 MOODY
Radio™